THE TEENAGER'S GUIDE TO FINANCIAL TRIUMPH:
FROM RAGS TO RICHES

FINANCIAL FREEDOM BLUEPRINT: 101 WEALTH-BUILDING PRINCIPLES FOR TEENAGERS

CHARUKA ABHAYAWICKRAMA

Published by
Aspire Capital Investments Pty Ltd
info@aspirecapitalinvestments.com.au
www.aspirecapitalinvestments.com.au

Aspire

ISBN-13: 978-0-6459311-1-2

Disclaimer: The content presented in this book is intended solely for general commentary and does not constitute advice. It is not the intention of this material to offer or imply professional guidance. Readers are strongly advised against making decisions solely based on the content within this book without first seeking and duly considering tailored professional advice in line with their unique circumstances. The application of the principles outlined herein lies solely within the discretion of the reader. Both the author and publisher hereby disclaim any and all liability, regardless of whether the reader has purchased this publication, for any actions taken or not taken, and the subsequent consequences thereof, by any individual relying in any capacity, whether entirely or partially, upon the entirety or specific portions of the contents contained in this publication.

Contents

About the Author

Hey, I'm Charuka Abhayawickrama, but just Charuka will do. At the sprightly age of 19, I caught a flight to Australia, driven by a hunger for knowledge and a dream to earn a university degree. In a matter of years, I found myself working alongside industry giants like APRA, Insurance Australia Group, and Commsec – arguably the top retail stock broker in the region. My entrepreneurial spirit led me to create, manage, and eventually sell a variety of businesses, ranging from bustling restaurants and lively pubs to specialized consultancy and software development firms.

By my 45th birthday, I kicked the traditional 9-to-5 to the curb. Why? Because I had built up enough passive income to overshadow any desk job out there. The secret sauce? A combination of savvy stock market investments I started at 15 and some smart property moves after I landed in Australia.

Have you come across the saying "shirtsleeves to shirtsleeves in three generations"? Essentially, it implies that while the first generation amasses wealth, the second sustains it, and the third might just squander it all away. I vowed not to let that happen to my lineage. I've passionately imparted my financial acumen to my teenage children, but admittedly, their digital age perspectives sometimes clash with my tried-and-tested methods. Phrases like "Dad, we just don't see money the way you do" often echo in our conversations. With the digital era ushering in financial advice through platforms like TikTok and Instagram, my old-school approach might seem a tad outmoded.

So, I wrote this book. Whether you're just like my teens, a little sceptical of 'old school' wisdom, or someone hungry for genuine financial insights, these principles are golden. I've made mistakes, paid the price, literally, but I hope you can sidestep those pitfalls. Remember, while money might not buy happiness directly, it sure does make a lot of other things accessible.

Financial literacy isn't a one-time lesson; it's a lifetime journey. Dive into these pages and arm yourself for a wealthy future. Let's make money moves together!

Preface

To the ambitious teenager reading this book, or perhaps the concerned parent eager for their child to grasp the intricacies of wealth and money management, welcome. Within the pages that follow lies the blueprint to navigating the turbulent waters of finance and harnessing them for a successful voyage.

So, why should you care about money stuff when you're still a teen? Think of it like this: If you want to build an awesome, super-tall tower, you've got to start with a solid base, right? Same thing with understanding money. Learn it early, and you'll be set for life.

This isn't just some boring money rulebook. "Rags to Riches: The Teenager's Handbook for Financial Success" is packed with experiences and lessons learnt from Charuka Abhayawickrama's own life—the good, the bad, and everything he learned along the way. Sure, times have changed with all the tech and social media stuff, but the basics of making it big? Those are still the same.

Consider this book your financial compass. Just as sailors of old would rely on the North Star to guide their voyages, so too can you lean on the wisdom contained herein to chart your path to financial success. Whether you're aiming to become an entrepreneur, seeking independence through passive income, or simply aiming to secure a comfortable future, this book will equip you with the tools and insights to make those dreams a reality.

Just a heads up: the money world can be tough. It takes time, hard work, and always being ready to learn. Even though there are loads of new ways to handle money these days, the main rules still apply.

Embark on this journey with an open mind and a resolute spirit. Learn from Charuka's decades of experience and his passion for financial literacy. Most importantly, remember that it's never too early, nor too late, to begin writing your own 'rags to riches' story.

Here's to your future of financial freedom and success. Dive in and let the transformation begin.

Introduction

Picture this: A world buzzing with influencers showing off their latest hauls, and everyone wanting that 'instant rich' magic. It's tempting, right? But here's the real tea: real wealth isn't just about the flash; it's about the grind, the strategy, and yeah, the hustle. "From Rags to Riches: The Teenager's Handbook for Financial Success" isn't just another book; it's your game plan. It's all about arming you, the cool, tech-forward, and dream-chasing teens, with the cheat codes to crack the money game.

Most finance books? They're busy talking to adults drowning in debts, bills, and more grown-up money mess. But this guide? It's all about YOU. With "Financial Freedom Blueprint: 101 Wealth-Building Principles for Teenagers", we're diving into money matters, but keeping it 100% relatable. Whether you're figuring out how to stash away cash from your first gig, thinking of diving into the stock market, or just curious about why everyone's obsessed with compound interest, we've got your back.

Yeah, starting on this money journey sounds big. But guess what? All those millionaires and big names? They started just like you, probably even younger. Flipping through these pages isn't just about learning; it's about leveling up, taking control, and plotting your empire. So, are you ready to draft the map to your financial kingdom? Let's do it, step by step, rule by rule. Let the games begin!

The power of compounding

Start early: The power of compounding is most effective when you begin investing early in life.

The power of compounding is a fundamental concept in finance and investing that allows money to grow exponentially over time. It refers to the process of earning interest or returns on an initial investment, and then reinvesting those earnings to generate even more returns. Over time, the effect of compounding can be quite remarkable, as the earnings from previous periods are added to the principal, creating a snowball effect.

Albert Einstein, the renowned physicist, recognized the power of compounding and supposedly referred to it as the "eighth wonder of the world":

Let's demonstrate the power of compounding using the example of Manhattan Island was purchased from the Native Americans by the Dutch in 1626 for goods worth $24, which would be equivalent to about $1,100 to $2,600 in today's money, accounting for inflation. Now, imagine if the Native Americans had invested that $24 in a relatively conservative investment that earned an average annual return of 7% over the next 395 years (from 1626 to 2021). Here's how the investment would have grown over time:

Year 1: $24 x 1.07 = $25.68

Year 10: $24 x (1.07)^10 = $57.97

Year 50: $24 x (1.07)^50 = $616.40

Year 100: $24 x (1.07)^100 = $6,621.84

Year 200: $24 x (1.07)^200 = $70,898.15

Year 300: $24 x (1.07)^300 = $759,470.66

Year 395: $24 x (1.07)^395 = $8,000,000,000,000
(approximately 8 trillion dollars)

As you can see, the initial investment of $24, with the power of compounding at an annual return of 7%, would have grown to an astonishing $8 trillion over 395 years. Considering American wealth is about $100 trillion $8 trillion is a significant amount.

This example illustrates the tremendous impact of compounding over long periods, and it highlights the importance of starting to invest early to take full advantage of this powerful concept.

Let's explore the power of compounding using an initial investment of $10,000 at an annual return of 7% over different time horizons. We'll also compare the growth of this investment to one where you contribute an additional $100 per month. Lets say you like to have nice milkshake or latte in a fancy café or like to have bubble tea. Lets say if one mug of those drinks cost $8 and if you have 3 per week. That's roughly $25 and per month it is $100. That's your extra $100 contribution

SCENARIO 1: INVESTING $10,000 AT 7% FOR DIFFERENT TIME HORIZONS

Year 1: $10,000 x 1.07 = $10,700

Year 5: $10,000 x (1.07)^5 = $14,887

Year 10: $10,000 x (1.07)^10 = $19,671

Year 50: $10,000 x (1.07)^50 = $294,570

As you can see, the value of the initial investment of $10,000 grows significantly over time due to compounding. The longer the investment is left to grow, the more pronounced the effect becomes. After 50 years, the investment would have grown to approximately $294,570, almost 30 times the initial amount.

SCENARIO 2: INVESTING $10,000 AT 7% WITH AN ADDITIONAL $100 PER MONTH

In this scenario, in addition to the initial investment of $10,000, you contribute an extra $100 per month to the investment.

Year 1: $10,000 x 1.07 + ($100 x 12) = $11,400

Year 5: [$10,000 x (1.07)^5] + [($100 x 12) x (1.07)^5 + ($100 x 12) x (1.07)^4 + ... + ($100 x 12) x (1.07)^1] = $22,936

Year 10: [$10,000 x (1.07)^10] + [($100 x 12) x (1.07)^10 + ($100 x 12) x (1.07)^9 + ... + ($100 x 12) x (1.07)^1] = $49,496

Year 50: [$10,000 x (1.07)^50] + [($100 x 12) x (1.07)^50 + ($100 x 12) x (1.07)^49 + ... + ($100 x 12) x (1.07)^1] = $1,334,310

Adding a consistent monthly contribution of $100 significantly accelerates the growth of the investment. After 50 years, the investment would have grown to approximately $1,334,310, which is over four times the value of the original investment without the additional contributions.

This example demonstrates the power of compounding, especially when combined with regular contributions. It highlights the importance of starting to invest early and consistently contributing to investments over time to benefit from the snowball effect of compounding.

Warren Buffett, one of the most successful investors of all time, emphasized the significance of compounding in building wealth:

> "The most powerful force in the universe is compound interest."

John C. Bogle, the founder of The Vanguard Group, highlighted the benefits of long-term investing and the magic of compounding:

> "The magic of compounding returns is truly the eighth wonder of the world."

Ray Dalio, the billionaire investor and founder of Bridgewater Associates, acknowledged the transformative nature of compounding:

> "Compound interest is the most powerful force in the universe. It is the most important thing in finance."

Benjamin Franklin, one of the founding fathers of the United States, commented on the impact of compounding in his writings:

> "Money makes money. And the money that money makes, makes money."

A small leak can sink a big ship

The phrase "a small leak can sink a big ship" holds a valuable lesson in both saving money and investment. In the context of personal finance, it emphasizes the importance of being mindful of even the smallest expenses or leaks in our finances, as they can have a significant impact on our overall financial well-being.

its easier to say when you spend money on something its only $5, its only $10. If you buy something you want but you don't need that's a waste of money. This is true specially in the early part of your life keeping the principle 01 in mind power of compounding these little expenses could come back to hurt you down the line. You may think your Spotify subscription of its only few dollars per month and I can afford that. Put that subscription fee through compounding formula and see how it can hurt you over 5 years, 10 year or 20-year period. That's huge. That alone can be the difference getting ahead or not being able to get ahead in life financially.

SAVING MONEY PERSPECTIVE:

From a saving money perspective, the saying advises us to be vigilant about our spending habits and avoid unnecessary expenses. Small, seemingly insignificant expenses, when accumulated over time, can add up to a substantial amount and affect our ability to save and build wealth. For example, buying a daily cup of expensive coffee, frequent dining out, or impulse purchases can slowly drain our savings.

The key is to identify these leaks and make conscious efforts to plug them. Creating a budget and tracking expenses can help identify areas where we can cut back and save more. By eliminating or reducing these small leaks, we can redirect those funds towards saving and investing, which will have a compounding effect over time and lead to greater financial security and growth.

INVESTMENT PERSPECTIVE:

In the realm of investments, the saying reminds us of the potential risks associated with neglecting small issues in our investment strategy. Ignoring small warning signs or not diversifying investments adequately can expose us to unnecessary risks, and over time, these seemingly minor issues can lead to significant losses in our investment portfolio.

To avoid this, it is essential to conduct thorough research and due diligence before making investment decisions. Diversifying investments across different asset classes and industries can help spread risk and safeguard against the potential impact of individual investment losses. Regularly reviewing and adjusting the investment portfolio as needed can also prevent a small issue from turning into a major financial setback.

In summary, the adage "a small leak can sink a big ship" serves as a powerful reminder to be mindful of the small details in our financial life, whether it's saving money or investing. By addressing these leaks proactively, we can ensure a stronger financial foundation and achieve our long-term financial goals.

The secret to financial freedom is simple: Spend less than you earn, invest the difference, and avoid debt.

Spend less than you earn, invest the difference, and avoid debt

The secret to financial freedom is simple: Spend less than you earn, invest the difference, and avoid debt.

This quote emphasizes the importance of living within your means, prioritizing saving and investing, and being cautious about taking on excessive debt. By consistently spending less than you earn and making wise financial decisions, you can gradually build wealth and work towards achieving financial freedom over time.

Remember that achieving financial freedom is a personal journey, and there is no one-size-fits-all approach. It requires discipline, patience, and a commitment to long-term financial planning. Setting clear financial goals, creating a budget, and being mindful of your spending habits are essential steps toward gaining control over your financial future and ultimately attaining financial freedom.

7 signs of achieving financial freedom include:

- Sufficient Savings and Investments: Achieving financial freedom typically involves accumulating enough savings and investments to cover one's living expenses, both in the short term and long term, without the need for constant income from work.

- Debt-Free or Manageable Debt: Being free from overwhelming debts is an essential part of financial freedom. Individuals strive to pay off high-interest debts and keep debt levels manageable.

- Passive Income Sources: Financially free individuals often have multiple streams of passive income, such as investments, rental properties, dividends, or other sources that generate income without requiring active work.

- Flexibility and Independence: Financial freedom allows individuals to have greater flexibility in their life choices. They can choose to work because they want to, not because they have to, and they can pursue passions, hobbies, or meaningful projects without financial constraints.

- Emergency Fund: Having an emergency fund is crucial for financial freedom. It provides a safety net to cover unexpected expenses without disrupting long-term financial plans

- Budgeting and Financial Planning: Being financially free requires effective budgeting and financial planning to ensure that expenses align with income and savings goals.

- Peace of Mind: Financial freedom brings a sense of security and peace of mind, knowing that one has the means to handle financial challenges and unexpected events.

Achieving financial freedom often requires discipline, prudent financial decisions, and a long-term perspective on managing finances. It is a journey that may take time, but with careful planning and perseverance, many individuals can work toward and eventually attain financial freedom.

Good debt versus Bad debt

RULE OF THUMB:

Good Debt: Good debt is typically considered as debt used to acquire assets that have the potential to appreciate in value or generate income. Examples include a mortgage on a property, student loans for education, or business loans to start or expand a profitable business.

Bad Debt: Bad debt refers to debt incurred to purchase items that do not appreciate in value and do not generate income. Examples include credit card debt for consumer goods, high-interest personal loans for vacations, or excessive car loans for luxury vehicles.

Quote:

> "The rich buy assets. The poor only have expenses.
> The middle class buys liabilities they think are assets."
> - Robert Kiyosaki, "Rich Dad Poor Dad"

This quote from Robert Kiyosaki encapsulates the idea that wealthy individuals tend to focus on acquiring assets that can generate wealth and provide future financial benefits. On the other hand, those with limited financial success often spend their money on items that do not contribute to their financial growth, mistaking liabilities for assets. The key is to understand the distinction between good and bad debt and use debt as a tool to build wealth rather than as a means of consumption.

Remember, not all debt is necessarily bad, but it's essential to assess how the debt will impact your financial situation and whether it aligns with your long-term financial goals. Good debt, when managed responsibly and strategically, can be a stepping stone towards financial prosperity and freedom.

The 50/30/20 Rule

The 50/30/20 Rule is a simple budgeting guideline that helps individuals allocate their after-tax income into three main categories: **needs, wants, and savings**. It provides a structured approach to managing finances and achieving a balance between essential expenses, discretionary spending, and saving for the future.

HERE'S A DETAILED BREAKDOWN OF THE 50/30/20 RULE:

50% for Needs:

This category includes essential expenses that are necessary for daily living and maintaining a stable lifestyle. It encompasses things you can't do without and must pay regularly. Some examples of needs include:

- Rent or mortgage payments
- Utilities (electricity, water, gas
- Groceries and essential food items
- Health insurance premiums
- Transportation costs (car payments, public transportation, fuel)
- Minimum debt payments (credit cards, student loans)

The goal is to ensure that these essential expenses do not exceed 50% of your after-tax income. Adjusting your lifestyle and reducing unnecessary expenses can be helpful if you find that your needs are taking up too much of your budget.

30% for Wants:

This category covers discretionary spending or non-essential expenses that enhance your lifestyle and provide enjoyment. These are things you desire but can live without if necessary. Examples of wants include:

- Dining out and entertainment
- Travel and vacations
- Cable or streaming services
- Shopping for non-essential items
- Hobbies and leisure activities

It's important to be mindful of your wants and avoid overspending in this category. While it's essential to enjoy life, keeping these expenses within 30% of your after-tax income ensures that you prioritize your long-term financial goals.

20% for Savings and Debt Repayment:

The last category is devoted to savings and investments for the future and debt repayment. This portion is critical for building wealth, preparing for emergencies, and reducing debt. Examples include:

- Retirement savings
- Emergency fund contributions
- Saving for major purchases (a house, a car)
- Additional debt payments (to pay off loans faster)
- Investments (stocks, mutual funds, etc.)

Allocating 20% of your after-tax income to savings and debt repayment helps ensure that you are making progress towards your financial goals and securing your financial future.

By following the 50/30/20 Rule, you create a structured budget that allows you to meet your essential needs, enjoy discretionary spending, and prioritize savings and debt reduction, ultimately improving your financial well-being. Remember that this rule can be adjusted based on individual circumstances, but the fundamental principle of balancing needs, wants, and savings remains essential.

PRINCIPLE 06

Mixing finances with friendships risks both wealth and relationship

Never borrow from friends and never lend to friends.

This is a cautionary Principle that advises against mixing personal relationships with financial transactions. While it may seem like a convenient solution in times of need or to help out a friend, there are several reasons why borrowing from or lending to friends can lead to potential problems and strained relationships:

⊙ Financial Strain and Risk: When you borrow money from a friend, you are putting financial strain on their resources, and if you are unable to repay on time or as agreed, it can create financial difficulties for your friend. Similarly, if you lend money to a friend, there's a risk that they may not be able to repay you, leading to a financial loss for you.

⊙ Lack of Formal Agreement: Unlike formal financial transactions, borrowing or lending among friends often lacks proper documentation and clear terms. Without a written agreement, misunderstandings can arise regarding the amount borrowed, the repayment schedule, or any interest involved.

⊙ Impact on the Relationship: Money matters can strain even the strongest of friendships. If there are delays or issues with repayment, it may cause tension and lead to resentment or damaged trust between friends.

- Different Financial Situations: Friends may have different financial situations, priorities, and budget constraints. Borrowing or lending money can create a significant disparity in financial positions and may lead to feelings of inequality or envy.

- Expectations and Boundaries: When money is involved, it can be challenging to maintain clear boundaries in a personal relationship. It may lead to uncomfortable situations, constant reminders, or even the risk of losing the friendship if the financial aspect becomes a point of contention.

Instead of borrowing from or lending to friends, it's better to consider alternative solutions:

- Personal Emergency Fund: Build and maintain an emergency fund to handle unexpected expenses and financial emergencies. Having your own safety net ensures you don't need to rely on others for financial help.

- Seek Professional Advice: If you are facing financial challenges, consider seeking advice from a financial advisor or counsellor who can help you explore other options for managing your situation.

- Alternative Lending Sources: If you need financial assistance, explore traditional lending options like banks, credit unions, or reputable online lenders. These institutions have structured processes and clear terms for borrowing.

- Support Without Money: Instead of lending money, consider offering support in non-monetary ways, such as providing emotional support, helping with job searches, or offering resources and connections.

Ultimately, while helping a friend in need is a noble intention, it's essential to approach financial matters with caution and prioritize the preservation of the friendship. Mixing finances with personal relationships can be risky, and it's crucial to maintain clear boundaries and communicate openly about money matters if such situations arise.

Rule of 72

The Rule of 72 is a simple and quick financial calculation that allows you to estimate how long it will take for your money to double at a fixed annual rate of return or interest. It is a useful tool for making approximate projections for investments and savings with compounded growth.

To use the Rule of 72, divide the number 72 by the annual rate of return (or interest) on your investment. The result will be the approximate number of years it will take for your initial investment to double.

Mathematically, the Rule of 72 can be expressed as follows:

Years to Double = 72 / Annual Rate of Return

where:

> "Years to Double" is the approximate time it takes for your investment to double.

> "Annual Rate of Return" is the annual interest rate or rate of return on your investment.

It's important to note that the Rule of 72 is a rough estimation and assumes a constant annual rate of return, which may not be the case in real-world investments that have fluctuating returns.

Here's an example to illustrate how the Rule of 72 works in a financial and investment context:

EXAMPLE 1: SAVING ACCOUNT INTEREST

Let's say you have money in a savings account that earns an annual interest rate of 4%. To calculate how long it will take for your savings to double:

Years to Double = 72 / Annual Interest Rate

Years to Double = 72 / 4 = 18 years

In this example, it will take approximately 18 years for your money in the savings account to double, assuming the interest rate remains constant.

EXAMPLE 2: INVESTMENT RETURN

Suppose you're considering investing in a mutual fund that historically has delivered an average annual return of 8%. Using the Rule of 72, you can estimate how long it might take for your investment to double:

Years to Double = 72 / Annual Rate of Return

Years to Double = 72 / 8 = 9 years

In this case, it would take approximately 9 years for your investment to double at an 8% average annual rate of return.

Overall, the Rule of 72 is a useful tool for gaining a quick understanding of the time it takes for your money to grow through compounding, and it can help you make informed financial decisions when evaluating different investment opportunities.

Differentiate Active and Passive Income

Understand the difference between active income (earned from your job) and passive income (earned from investments or businesses).

ACTIVE INCOME:

Active income refers to money earned through direct, ongoing efforts and the exchange of time and skills. This income is typically generated from active involvement in work or business activities. Active income requires active participation, and when you stop working or providing services, the income stops.

Examples of Active Income:

- Salary from a job: Money earned by working for an employer or company.
- Self-employment income: Income generated by running a business or freelancing.
- Hourly wages: Earnings based on an hourly rate for services rendered.
- Commission-based income: Income earned based on sales or referrals.

PASSIVE INCOME:

Passive income is money earned with minimal effort or direct involvement after the initial setup or investment. It's income generated from assets or ventures that continue to produce returns without constant active effort. Passive income provides a level of financial freedom because it allows individuals to earn money without being tied to a specific job or location.

Examples of Passive Income:

- Rental income: Earnings from real estate properties or land leased to tenants.
- Dividend income: Income received from owning shares of dividend-paying stocks.
- Royalties: Income earned from the use of intellectual property, like books, music, or patents.
- Affiliate marketing income: Earnings from promoting and selling products or services online.
- Income from automated businesses or websites.

DIFFERENTIATION:

The key difference between active and passive income lies in the level of effort and ongoing involvement required to earn money. Active income necessitates active participation, while passive income involves setting up income streams that continue to generate money with limited effort after the initial work.

Building Wealth and Achieving Financial Freedom:

Both active and passive income can contribute to building wealth and achieving financial freedom, but they have different implications for your financial journey:

ACTIVE INCOME:

Active income is usually the primary source of income for most people, especially when starting their careers. It provides immediate cash flow to cover living expenses and allows for saving and investing.

To build wealth with active income, individuals can focus on increasing their skills, getting promotions, or starting businesses. This can lead to higher earnings and the ability to save more for investments.

The challenge with active income is that it's time-bound, and the income stops when you stop working. Achieving financial freedom may require diversifying income sources and creating passive income streams.

PASSIVE INCOME:

Passive income is an essential component of achieving financial freedom. It can supplement active income and provide ongoing revenue, even if you're not actively working.

Building passive income streams often requires initial effort, such as investing in real estate, building a successful online business, or creating intellectual property.

Once established, passive income can continue to grow, and the combined effect of multiple passive income streams can lead to financial independence and the ability to pursue other interests without relying solely on active work.

In summary, a combination of active and passive income can significantly impact your journey towards building wealth and achieving financial freedom. While active income provides immediate cash flow and stability, passive income offers the potential for long-term financial security and the freedom to pursue a more balanced and fulfilling life. Diversifying income sources and investing wisely in both active and passive ventures can contribute to your financial success and overall well-being.

Create Multiple Income Streams

Diversify your income sources to reduce dependence on a single stream and increase financial security. Creating multiple income streams refers to the practice of generating income from various sources, beyond just a single job or business. It involves diversifying your income sources to have multiple streams of cash flow, which can enhance financial stability, increase overall income, and contribute to building wealth.

EXAMPLE 1 - MULTIPLE STREAMS OF ACTIVE INCOME:

John works as a marketing executive in a company and also runs a small graphic design business on the side. He earns a salary from his job and additional income from his freelance graphic design projects. By having multiple streams of active income, John can increase his earnings and save more money for investments or savings goals.

EXAMPLE 2 - COMBINATION OF ACTIVE AND PASSIVE INCOME:

Sarah is a real estate agent and earns a commission for each property sale. In addition to her active income, Sarah also invests in rental properties. The rental income provides a passive income stream that continues to grow even when she's not actively involved in selling properties. This combination of active and passive income allows Sarah to achieve financial freedom faster.

DIVERSIFY YOUR INCOME SOURCES:

Diversification of income sources involves spreading your earnings across different types of income streams. This strategy helps reduce reliance on a single source of income, mitigates risks associated with economic fluctuations or job instability, and enhances overall financial security.

EXAMPLE 1 - DIVERSIFICATION IN INVESTMENTS:

Lisa diversifies her investment portfolio by investing in various asset classes like stocks, term deposits, real estate, and managed funds. By not putting all her money in one investment type, Lisa reduces the impact of market volatility and increases the potential for consistent returns from different sources.

EXAMPLE 2 - DIVERSIFICATION IN BUSINESS VENTURES:

Tom is an entrepreneur who owns a chain of restaurants. To diversify his business income, he decides to start a catering service and invests in a food delivery app. By doing so, Tom reduces the risk of relying solely on restaurant sales and creates multiple income streams within the food industry.

It's important to note that creating multiple income streams and diversifying your income requires thoughtful planning, time, effort, and sometimes initial capital investment. The key is to identify opportunities that align with your skills, interests, and financial goals. Over time, a well-executed strategy for multiple income streams can significantly contribute to your journey towards wealth creation and financial freedom.

Save Regularly

Develop a habit of saving a portion of your income regularly. Even small contributions can add up over time.

Saving regularly is a fundamental and essential practice in wealth creation and achieving financial freedom. It involves consistently setting aside a portion of your income and putting it into savings or investments. The power of regular saving lies in its ability to accumulate wealth gradually over time through the magic of compound interest and consistent contributions.

IMPORTANCE OF SAVING REGULARLY:

1. Building Wealth: Regular saving allows you to accumulate money and build wealth over time. Even small contributions, when consistently made, can grow significantly over the long term.

2. Financial Security: Having savings provides a safety net for unexpected expenses or emergencies, reducing the need to rely on debt during difficult times.

3. Financial Independence: Regular saving helps you achieve financial independence by creating a pool of assets that can generate passive income or support your lifestyle during retirement.

4. Compound Interest: The longer you save and invest, the more time your money has to grow through compounding.

Over time, your earnings can generate additional returns, leading to exponential growth.

EXAMPLES OF REGULAR SAVING:

1. Automated Savings: Set up automatic transfers from your checking account to a savings account or investment account every month. This ensures that you save consistently without the need for manual efforts.
2. Paying Yourself First: Treat your savings as an essential expense. Allocate a fixed percentage of your income as savings before paying other bills or expenses.
3. Windfall Savings: Whenever you receive unexpected money, such as a bonus, tax refund, or gift, consider saving a portion of it instead of spending it all.
4. Small Lifestyle Adjustments: Look for opportunities to save money in your daily life. For example, bring lunch to work instead of eating out, cancel unnecessary subscriptions, or find more affordable alternatives for regular expenses.

Regular saving plays a crucial role in building wealth and achieving financial freedom:

1. Accumulating Capital: Regular contributions to savings and investments allow you to accumulate capital, which can be used for various financial goals, such as buying a home, starting a business, or retiring comfortably.
2. Risk Management: Having savings acts as a safety net during challenging times, reducing the need to take on debt or sell assets at unfavourable prices.
3. Financial Discipline: Cultivating the habit of saving regularly instils financial discipline and responsibility, making you more conscious of your spending habits and financial decisions.

4. Long-Term Vision: Regular saving encourages a long-term perspective on financial planning. It helps you stay committed to your goals and resist impulsive spending.

Saving regularly is a cornerstone of financial success. By developing this habit and consistently contributing to your savings and investments, you can create a solid foundation for wealth creation, attain financial security, and work towards achieving the dream of financial freedom. Remember, every little bit saved adds up, and starting early gives your money more time to grow and compound, increasing the potential for long-term financial prosperity.

PRINCIPLE 11

Set Financial Goals

Define clear financial goals, both short-term and long-term, and work towards achieving them.

Setting financial goals is a fundamental step towards wealth creation and achieving financial freedom, especially for the teenage generation. Goals provide a clear direction and motivation to work towards a financially secure future. When you set financial goals, you learn valuable lessons about budgeting, saving, investing, and prioritizing their spending, which are essential skills for building wealth over time.

HERE'S HOW YOU CAN EFFECTIVELY SET FINANCIAL GOALS TO YOUR WAY TOWARDS FINANCIAL SUCCESS:

1. Short-term Goals: Let's start with short-term goals that we can achieve within a few weeks or months. For example, saving some money from our allowance or earnings or creating a budget for a specific event or something we want to buy. When we reach these short-term goals, we'll feel awesome and be pumped to tackle bigger ones!

2. Medium-term Goals: These goals might take a bit longer, like several months to a couple of years. You could save up for a cool new phone or a laptop, fund an epic school trip, or build an emergency fund for those unexpected

moments. Setting deadlines for these goals will help you stay on track.

3. Long-term Goals: Dream big with long-term goals! They might take several years to achieve, but they're totally worth it. It could be saving for higher education, buying a car, or even saving up for a future home. These goals will need dedication and might involve more complicated financial planning and investing.

4. Be Specific and Measurable: Instead of vague goals like "I want to save money," let's be specific and set measurable targets. Like saying, "I want to save $500 by the end of the year." This way, you can track our progress easily.

5. Be Realistic: Let's set goals that are doable based on our current financial situation. Unrealistic goals can be frustrating, so let's aim for things we know we can achieve. When we reach these goals, we'll feel awesome and motivated to aim higher.

6. Set Deadlines: Give each goal a deadline to create a sense of urgency and avoid procrastination. We can check in regularly to see how we're doing and make changes if needed.

7. Pay off Debts: If we have any debts, it's crucial to prioritize paying them off as part of our goals. High-interest debts can be a burden, so let's tackle them first.

8. Learn About Investing: Investing might sound intimidating, but it's powerful! We can start small and set a goal to invest some money regularly. Over time, it'll grow and help us build wealth.

9. Stay Flexible: Life changes, and so can our goals. Let's be open to adjusting them as needed. Our dreams and circumstances might change, and that's totally okay!

10. Ask for Help: Don't be shy to seek guidance from parents, teachers, or financial advisors. Having someone experienced to support us can make a big difference.

By setting clear, achievable financial goals, we'll develop good money habits early on, setting us up for a successful financial future. Achieving these goals will teach us discipline, responsibility, and control over our finances – all things that lead to financial freedom. So let's take charge of our money and start working towards our dreams! We've got this!

Health is wealth

Taking care of physical and mental well-being is crucial for long-term success. Encourage teenagers to adopt a healthy lifestyle, prioritize mental health, and practice mindfulness. A healthy body and mind contribute to better decision-making, productivity, and overall well-being, which are all vital components of financial success.

IMPORTANCE OF HEALTH AND WELL-BEING IN WEALTH CREATION:

1. Longevity and Career Success: Maintaining good physical and mental health can lead to a longer and more productive career. When you are healthy, you are better equipped to excel in your job or business, leading to higher earnings and increased opportunities for wealth creation.

2. Reducing Medical Expenses: Prioritizing health can help prevent or manage health issues, reducing the financial burden of medical expenses. By investing in preventive care and healthy lifestyle choices, you can save money on healthcare costs in the long run.

3. Better Financial Decision-making: When you are physically and mentally well, you are more likely to make sound financial decisions. A clear and focused mind allows you to analyse opportunities, assess risks, and stay disciplined in your financial strategies.

4. Productivity and Time Management: Good health enhances productivity and time management skills. By maintaining high energy levels and mental clarity, you can be more efficient in your work and free up time for personal growth and wealth-building activities.

EXAMPLES OF HEALTH AND WEALTH CONNECTION:

1. Healthy Lifestyle for Career Growth: Sarah, a young professional, maintains a healthy lifestyle by exercising regularly, eating nutritious food, and getting enough sleep. Her physical and mental well-being help her excel in her job, leading to promotions and salary increases. As a result, she can save more and invest in various wealth-building opportunities.

2. Preventing Costly Health Issues: John, a middle-aged entrepreneur, prioritizes his health by going for regular health check-ups and leading an active lifestyle. As a result, he can avoid serious health issues that could have been costly to treat. The money he saves on potential medical expenses can be channelled into investments for his future financial security.

3. Mindfulness and Financial Decisions: Alex practices mindfulness through meditation and self-reflection. This habit helps him stay calm and focused during market fluctuations, preventing impulsive financial decisions. His disciplined approach to investing leads to better returns and overall financial success.

Health and well-being are essential foundations for wealth creation and achieving financial freedom. Taking care of your physical and mental health contributes to better financial decision-making, reduces healthcare expenses, and enhances productivity in your career or business. Encouraging teenagers and young adults to prioritize their health sets them on a path of long-term success and financial prosperity. By understanding that health truly is wealth, individuals can make informed choices that lead to a balanced and fulfilling life, both financially and personally.

Master your finances through mindful budgeting

Budgeting is a fundamental and powerful tool that plays a crucial role in building and managing wealth. Budgeting is not just about limiting spending; it is a strategic approach to allocate financial resources efficiently and purposefully. By creating a budget, individuals can control their finances, optimize savings, and direct funds towards wealth-building opportunities, ultimately leading to financial success and the achievement of long-term financial goals.

KEY ASPECTS OF BUDGETING FOR WEALTH CREATION:

1. Financial Awareness and Control: Budgeting provides a clear picture of your income, expenses, and cash flow. This awareness allows you to take control of your finances, make informed decisions, and identify areas where you can cut back on unnecessary expenses.

2. Prioritizing Savings and Investments: Budgeting ensures that a portion of your income is allocated to savings and investments consistently. Regularly contributing to savings and investment accounts allows your money to grow over time through compounding, leading to accelerated wealth creation.

3. Debt Reduction and Elimination: A well-structured budget can help you allocate extra funds to pay off debts

strategically. By reducing high-interest debt, you free up more money for investments and saving, improving your overall financial position.

4. Identifying Wealth-Building Opportunities: Budgeting allows you to set aside funds for specific wealth-building opportunities, such as starting a business, investing in real estate, or participating in the stock market. These investments can generate passive income and increase your net worth over time.

5. Minimizing Financial Stress: By sticking to a budget, you avoid overspending and financial strain. This reduces stress related to money matters and allows you to focus on wealth-building strategies with a clear mind.

EXAMPLE OF BUDGETING FOR WEALTH CREATION:

Let's consider Natasha, who wants to build wealth and achieve financial independence. She creates a budget to track her income and expenses. After analysing her spending habits, she identifies areas where she can cut back on non-essential expenses, such as dining out and entertainment. Natasha reallocates those savings into her investment account and retirement fund. Over time, her investments grow, generating passive income that contributes to her financial freedom.

Budgeting is a powerful wealth creation tool that provides financial control, discipline, and direction. By creating a budget and sticking to it, individuals can optimize their savings, reduce debt, and make intentional financial decisions that lead to long-term wealth creation and financial freedom. Budgeting is not restrictive; instead, it empowers individuals to take charge of their financial journey and work towards their financial aspirations with clarity and purpose.

Emergency Fund: Safeguarding Your Finances Against the Unexpected

An emergency fund is a financial safety net that provides funds to cover unexpected expenses or emergencies without relying on credit cards or loans. It acts as a buffer against financial setbacks, such as medical emergencies, car repairs, or sudden job loss. Having an emergency fund is a crucial step in achieving financial stability and avoiding unnecessary consumer debts. It not only safeguards against financial crises but also provides peace of mind and paves the way for wealth creation and financial freedom.

AVOIDING CONSUMER DEBTS:

1. Preventing Debt Accumulation: An emergency fund helps avoid the need to rely on credit cards or personal loans to cover unforeseen expenses. Without an emergency fund, people often resort to borrowing, leading to high-interest debts that can be challenging to repay.

2. Preserving Credit Score: Using an emergency fund instead of consumer debts protects your credit score. A strong credit score is vital for accessing favourable interest rates on loans and other financial opportunities.

3. Breaking the Debt Cycle: Having an emergency fund breaks the cycle of living pay check to pay check and getting trapped in a perpetual cycle of debt. By covering unexpected expenses from savings, individuals can focus on debt reduction and wealth-building strategies.

PEACE OF MIND AND FINANCIAL SECURITY:

1. Reduced Stress: Knowing that you have an emergency fund provides a sense of security and reduces financial stress. You are better prepared to handle unforeseen circumstances, fostering emotional well-being.
2. Flexibility in Decision-Making: With an emergency fund in place, you can make financial decisions more confidently. For example, you may be more open to career changes or entrepreneurial pursuits without the fear of immediate financial crisis.
3. Protecting Long-Term Goals: An emergency fund protects your long-term financial goals from being derailed by unexpected expenses. It allows you to continue investing in wealth-building opportunities without interruption.

WEALTH CREATION AND FINANCIAL FREEDOM:

1. Stability for Investments: An emergency fund acts as a safety cushion, allowing you to invest without worrying about sudden liquidity needs. This stability enables you to pursue long-term investments with confidence.
2. Opportunity for Risk-Taking: With an emergency fund, you can take calculated risks in investments or entrepreneurial ventures. Knowing you have a financial safety net mitigates the fear of failure.

3. Accelerating Wealth Growth: By avoiding consumer debts and having an emergency fund, you can direct more money toward investments, savings, and debt reduction. This accelerates the growth of your net worth and moves you closer to financial freedom.

Building an emergency fund is a critical step in achieving financial stability and avoiding consumer debts. It provides peace of mind, financial security, and the flexibility to pursue wealth-building opportunities. An emergency fund empowers individuals to handle unexpected expenses with confidence, protect their long-term financial goals, and take the necessary risks for accelerated wealth creation and the journey towards financial freedom.

Navigating Financial Wellness Through Wise Debt Handling

Debt management is a vital component of wealth creation and achieving financial freedom. It involves adopting strategies to minimize debt, use debt responsibly, and ensure that debt obligations are manageable within one's financial capacity. Wisely managing debt is crucial for avoiding financial stress, safeguarding long-term financial goals, and building a solid foundation for financial success.

IMPORTANCE OF DEBT MANAGEMENT FOR WEALTH CREATION:

1. Reducing Financial Stress: High levels of debt can lead to financial stress and anxiety. By managing debt wisely, individuals can maintain better control over their finances and reduce the burden of debt-related pressures.

2. Preserving Cash Flow: Excessive debt repayments can hinder cash flow and limit the ability to invest and save. Effective debt management ensures that debt repayments remain manageable, freeing up more money for wealth-building activities.

3. Protecting Credit Score: Responsible debt management helps maintain a healthy credit score. A good credit score is essential for accessing favourable interest rates on loans and other financial opportunities.

4. Preventing Excessive Interest Payments: Minimizing debt and using low-interest debt strategically can significantly reduce the amount of interest paid over time. This helps preserve wealth and accelerates financial growth.

STRATEGIES FOR DEBT MANAGEMENT:

1. Budgeting and Prioritizing Debt Payments: Create a budget that allocates a portion of your income to debt repayments. Prioritize high-interest debts to minimize interest payments and pay off debts faster.

2. Avoiding High-Interest Debt: Minimize the use of high-interest debt, such as credit card debt. Whenever possible, opt for lower interest options or consider using savings instead of borrowing.

3. Consolidating Debt: Consider debt consolidation if it results in a lower overall interest rate and simplifies debt management. However, be cautious not to accumulate more debt during the consolidation process.

4. Negotiating with Creditors: If facing financial challenges, reach out to creditors to discuss alternative repayment arrangements. They may offer temporary relief or adjusted repayment plans to ease the burden.

IMPACT ON WEALTH CREATION:

1. Accelerated Savings and Investments: Effective debt management frees up more money for savings and investments. This accelerates wealth creation and moves individuals closer to achieving financial freedom.

2. Reduced Dependence on Debt: Wisely managing debt reduces reliance on borrowing to cover expenses,

preserving financial stability and avoiding the pitfalls of debt dependency.

3. Opportunities for Investment: By minimizing debt, individuals can confidently take advantage of investment opportunities without worrying about debt obligations hindering their financial decisions.

EXAMPLE:

Sarah decides to manage her debt wisely to achieve financial freedom. She pays off high-interest credit card debt aggressively while continuing to make affordable monthly payments on her student loans. As a result, she clears her credit card debt within a year, saving a significant amount in interest payments. With the extra cash flow, Sarah starts contributing more to her retirement fund and invests in a diversified portfolio. Over time, her investments grow, and she is able to achieve financial freedom ahead of her initial target.

Debt management is a crucial aspect of wealth creation and achieving financial freedom. By minimizing and managing debt wisely, individuals can reduce financial stress, preserve cash flow, and protect their long-term financial goals. Effective debt management empowers individuals to make informed financial decisions, accelerates savings and investments, and paves the way for a secure and prosperous financial future.

Avoid lifestyle inflation: Resist increasing expenses as income rises

Avoiding lifestyle inflation is a key principle in wealth creation and achieving financial freedom. Lifestyle inflation refers to the tendency of increasing one's spending and expenses as income rises. While it's natural to want to enjoy the benefits of higher income, succumbing to lifestyle inflation can hinder wealth-building efforts and delay financial independence. Instead, adopting a frugal and intentional approach to spending can free up more resources for saving, investing, and pursuing long-term financial goals.

IMPORTANCE OF AVOIDING LIFESTYLE INFLATION FOR WEALTH CREATION:

1. Accelerating Savings: By keeping expenses in check and resisting lifestyle inflation, individuals can allocate a larger portion of their income to savings. This increased savings rate can accelerate wealth creation over time.

2. Building Investment Capital: Avoiding lifestyle inflation provides more capital for investments. By directing funds into investment vehicles, individuals can grow their wealth and generate passive income streams for financial security.

3.   Reducing Financial Stress: Keeping lifestyle expenses stable despite income increases reduces financial stress. A lower financial burden allows for greater peace of mind and focus on long-term financial objectives.

4.   Protecting Against Uncertainty: A frugal lifestyle and controlled expenses can act as a safety net during economic downturns or unexpected life events. Financial flexibility provides security in times of uncertainty.

STRATEGIES TO AVOID LIFESTYLE INFLATION:

1.   Stick to a Budget: Create and maintain a budget that reflects your financial goals and priorities. Use it to track expenses and ensure that spending aligns with your values and long-term aspirations.

2.   Automate Savings and Investments: Set up automatic transfers to savings and investment accounts. This ensures that a portion of your income goes towards building wealth before you have a chance to spend it.

3.   Avoid Impulse Purchases: Give yourself time to consider whether a purchase aligns with your needs and goals. Delaying non-essential purchases can prevent impulsive spending and unnecessary lifestyle inflation.

4.   Focus on Experiences over Material Possessions: Allocate funds to experiences, travel, and personal growth rather than accumulating material possessions. Experiences often bring lasting happiness, while material possessions may lead to further desire for upgrades.

IMPACT ON WEALTH CREATION AND FINANCIAL FREEDOM:

1.   Increased Investment Opportunities: Resisting lifestyle inflation provides more capital for investments. Over

time, compound growth can significantly increase wealth and passive income.

2.   Shorter Path to Financial Freedom: By avoiding unnecessary expenses, individuals can reach their financial independence goals faster. The increased savings rate expedites the accumulation of wealth.

3.   Financial Security: A disciplined approach to spending and avoiding lifestyle inflation creates a strong financial foundation. This stability protects against unexpected events and provides a sense of security.

EXAMPLE:

John, after receiving a promotion with a higher salary, decides not to succumb to lifestyle inflation. Instead, he continues to live within his previous budget and directs the additional income into retirement accounts and investments. Over time, his investments grow, and he achieves financial freedom earlier than his peers who increased their spending with each raise.

Avoiding lifestyle inflation is a powerful strategy in wealth creation and achieving financial freedom. By resisting the urge to increase expenses as income rises, individuals can accelerate savings, build investment capital, reduce financial stress, and protect against uncertainty. Prioritizing long-term financial goals over immediate gratification sets the stage for a more secure and prosperous financial future.

Diversify your investments

Spread your investments across different assets to reduce risk.

Diversification involves spreading investments across different asset classes and investment vehicles to minimize risk and increase the potential for long-term growth. By diversifying wisely, one can protect their capital from extreme fluctuations in any single investment and create a robust portfolio that aligns with their financial goals.

IMPORTANCE OF INVESTMENT DIVERSIFICATION:

1. Risk Mitigation: Diversifying investments helps reduce the impact of market volatility on the overall portfolio. Different assets tend to perform differently under various economic conditions, providing a buffer against losses.

2. Enhanced Growth Potential: By diversifying, teenagers can tap into various investment opportunities with different growth potentials. Some assets may have higher returns during specific periods, helping to boost overall portfolio performance.

3. Capital Preservation: Diversification protects the capital from significant losses. Even if one investment underperforms, other assets can balance the portfolio and prevent substantial wealth erosion.

4. Learning Experience: Embracing diversification early in life exposes teenagers to different investment concepts and

asset classes. This early education can set a solid foundation for informed financial decision-making as they progress through life.

STRATEGIES FOR INVESTMENT DIVERSIFICATION:

1. Asset Allocation: Allocate investments across different asset classes, such as stocks, bonds, real estate, and cash equivalents. Each asset class has unique risk and return characteristics.
2. Geographical Diversification: Consider investing in international markets in addition to domestic ones. This provides exposure to different economic conditions and reduces country-specific risks.
3. Individual Stocks and Funds: Invest in individual stocks of companies you believe in, but also consider diversifying through mutual funds or exchange-traded funds (ETFs) that hold a broad range of stocks.
4. Rebalance Periodically: Regularly review your portfolio and rebalance it to maintain the desired asset allocation. Rebalancing ensures that your investments stay aligned with your risk tolerance and financial goals.

IMPACT ON WEALTH CREATION AND FINANCIAL FREEDOM:

1. Consistent Growth: Diversification reduces the impact of market volatility, leading to more consistent and predictable portfolio growth over the long term.
2. Reduced Losses: By spreading investments across different assets, teenagers can protect their wealth from significant losses during market downturns.
3. Financial Independence: Diversification increases the probability of achieving financial freedom as a balanced

portfolio is less vulnerable to severe market swings that can delay reaching financial goals.

EXAMPLE:

Amy, a teenager interested in investing, diversifies her portfolio by investing in a mix of stocks, bonds, and a real estate investment trust (REIT). During a market downturn, while her stock investments may experience declines, her bonds and REIT investment continue to provide stability and income. Over time, the diversification of her portfolio helps Amy achieve steady growth and financial independence.

Diversifying investments is a vital strategy for teenagers aiming at wealth creation and achieving financial freedom. By spreading investments across different asset classes, teenagers can protect their capital, enjoy more consistent growth, and increase the likelihood of reaching their financial goals. Early adoption of diversification as an investment principle sets teenagers on a path towards financial success and a well-structured portfolio that can weather the ups and downs of the market over time.

Avoid impulse buying

Practice delayed gratification and think before making purchases.

Avoiding impulse buying is a critical habit to cultivate. Impulse buying refers to making spontaneous and unplanned purchases without carefully considering the necessity or long-term impact on one's finances. Practicing delayed gratification and taking the time to think before making purchases can lead to more intentional spending, increased savings, and a stronger foundation for building wealth.

IMPORTANCE OF AVOIDING IMPULSE BUYING FOR WEALTH CREATION AND INVESTING:

1. Financial Discipline: Avoiding impulse buying requires discipline and self-control. By developing this skill, individuals can resist unnecessary spending, allowing them to allocate more money towards investments and savings.

2. Enhanced Savings Rate: Practicing delayed gratification frees up funds for saving and investing. These extra savings can be channelled into wealth-building opportunities, accelerating the path to financial independence.

3. Reduced Debt: Impulse buying often leads to accumulating unnecessary debt. By curbing impulsive spending, individuals can avoid credit card debts and other liabilities, which hinder wealth accumulation.

4. Improved Investment Decisions: Taking time to think before making purchases extends to investment decisions as well. Making thoughtful, well-researched investment choices leads to more successful outcomes in the financial markets.

STRATEGIES TO AVOID IMPULSE BUYING:

1. Create a Shopping List: Before shopping, make a list of essential items and stick to it. Avoid deviating from the list unless it's for well-considered reasons.
2. Set Financial Goals: Establish clear financial goals and remind yourself of them regularly. Focusing on your long-term objectives can help resist the temptation of impulse buying.
3. Practice the 24-Hour Rule: When considering non-essential purchases, wait 24 hours before making the decision. This gives you time to evaluate whether the purchase is genuinely necessary or merely a fleeting desire.
4. Avoid Emotional Shopping: Be mindful of emotional triggers that may lead to impulse buying, such as stress, boredom, or retail therapy. Find alternative ways to cope with emotions rather than shopping.

IMPACT ON WEALTH CREATION AND INVESTING:

1. Increased Investment Capital: By avoiding impulse purchases, individuals can allocate more money towards investments, leading to greater capital growth and potential for long-term wealth accumulation.
2. Accelerated Debt Repayment: Curbing impulse spending reduces the likelihood of accumulating debt. This allows

individuals to focus on paying off existing debts, freeing up even more money for investments.

3. Building a Thoughtful Portfolio: Practicing thoughtful decision-making extends to investment choices. Investors who carefully research and analyse investment options are more likely to build a diversified and successful investment portfolio.

EXAMPLE:

Emma, a young investor, is tempted to buy the latest smartphone impulsively. However, she practices delayed gratification and decides to wait for a week before making the purchase. During that time, she realizes that her current smartphone meets all her needs, and the latest model would not significantly improve her daily life. Emma decides to prioritize investing the money instead, contributing it to her investment account. Over time, her disciplined approach to spending and investing leads to substantial wealth growth.

Avoiding impulse buying and practicing delayed gratification are essential for wealth creation and successful investing. By exercising financial discipline and carefully considering purchases, individuals can increase their savings rate, reduce debt, and build a thoughtful investment portfolio. This habit sets the stage for long-term financial success, allowing individuals to reach their financial goals more efficiently and achieve greater financial freedom.

"Save now and buy later" versus "Buy now, pay later"

The choice between "Save now and buy later" versus "Buy now, pay later" reflects two different approaches to managing your finances and achieving wealth-building and financial freedom.

Save Now and Buy Later: This approach involves prioritizing saving money before making a purchase. Instead of immediately buying something you want, you set aside money over time until you have enough saved to afford the item without going into debt. This approach is rooted in the principles of delayed gratification and responsible financial planning.

ADVANTAGES:

1. **Avoiding Debt:** By saving up for a purchase, you avoid taking on debt, which means you won't be burdened with interest payments or potential financial stress.
2. **Building Discipline:** Practicing delayed gratification helps build discipline and self-control, which are valuable skills in managing your overall financial life.
3. **Financial Security:** Saving money allows you to establish an emergency fund and build a safety net for unexpected expenses.

4. **Reduced Stress:** Without the pressure of immediate payments or debt, you can experience reduced financial stress and enjoy peace of mind.

DISADVANTAGES:

1. **Time and Patience:** Saving money takes time, which might delay your ability to acquire certain items or experiences.
2. **Opportunity Cost:** While you're saving for a particular purchase, you might miss out on time-sensitive opportunities or deals.

Buy Now, Pay Later: This approach involves acquiring what you want immediately by utilizing credit options, such as credit cards or instalment plans. Instead of paying the full amount upfront, you agree to pay the cost over a specified period. While this can provide instant gratification, it comes with potential financial risks if not managed carefully.

ADVANTAGES:

1. **Immediate Access:** You can enjoy the desired item or experience without having to wait or save up.
2. **Convenience:** Buy now, pay later options offer convenience and flexibility, allowing you to spread payments over time.
3. **Credit Building:** Responsible use of credit can contribute to building a positive credit history if payments are made on time.

DISADVANTAGES:

1. **Debt and Interest:** If not managed properly, buying now and paying later can lead to debt accumulation and interest payments, which can erode your overall wealth over time.

2. **Overspending:** The availability of credit might tempt you to overspend, leading to financial strain and potential difficulty in meeting payment obligations.

3. **Risk of Impulse Buying:** The immediate gratification can lead to impulse purchases, which might not align with your long-term financial goals.

4. **Financial Stress:** If multiple buy now, pay later obligations pile up, they can lead to financial stress and negatively impact your overall financial well-being.

In the context of building wealth and achieving financial freedom, the "Save now and buy later" approach aligns more closely with responsible financial management. By prioritizing saving, you can avoid debt, build a strong financial foundation, and work towards your long-term goals. However, there might be instances where carefully selected buy now, pay later options can be used judiciously, especially for items that hold value or contribute to personal or professional growth. The key is to strike a balance and make informed decisions that align with your financial objectives.

Consumer debt is a thief that steals your future earnings

Limit borrowing for consumption and focus on using credit for productive investments.

When you accumulate consumer debt, such as credit card debt or personal loans for non-essential purchases, you're essentially borrowing money to fund your current lifestyle. However, this comes at a cost – the interest you have to pay on the borrowed money. This interest can significantly add up over time, eating into your future earnings and the money you could have used to build wealth.

Example: Imagine you use a credit card to buy the latest gadgets, clothes, and other items that depreciate in value quickly. If you only make minimum payments, the interest on the unpaid balance accumulates, and you end up paying much more for these items than their original price. This means you're essentially losing money to interest payments, preventing you from allocating those funds toward more productive purposes.

PRIORITIZE CREDIT FOR APPRECIATING INVESTMENTS:

On the other hand, using credit for investments that appreciate in value can be a strategic way to leverage borrowed money for wealth creation. Appreciating investments have the potential to grow over time, generating returns that exceed the cost of borrowing. This allows you to build wealth and enhance your financial position.

Example: Consider investing in real estate. By using credit to finance a property purchase, you can potentially benefit from property value appreciation, rental income, and tax advantages. The income and value generated by the investment could outweigh the interest and borrowing costs, leading to positive financial outcomes.

In essence, this principle advises against using credit for items that lose value quickly (depreciate) and encourages using credit for assets or investments that have the potential to increase in value over time (appreciate). This mindset helps you make thoughtful decisions about how you use credit to enhance your financial well-being, focusing on long-term wealth creation rather than short-term consumption.

To achieve financial freedom, it's crucial to minimize consumer debt, manage your credit wisely, and prioritize investments that align with your financial goals. By doing so, you can break free from the cycle of borrowing to fund consumption and instead use credit as a tool to build a stronger financial foundation and work towards the life you envision.

Invest in learning today for a wealthier tomorrow

Taking an active interest in educating yourself about finance and investments is a critical step towards creating wealth and achieving financial freedom. Here's a more detailed explanation with relevant examples:

EMPOWERMENT THROUGH KNOWLEDGE:

The journey to financial independence begins with a commitment to self-education. By consistently learning about various investment options, financial markets, and personal finance strategies, you equip yourself with the knowledge needed to make informed decisions that will shape your financial future.

Example 1 - Investment Options:

Consider someone who is eager to grow their wealth over time. They begin by learning about the different investment vehicles available, such as stocks, bonds, real estate, and mutual funds. Armed with this knowledge, they can tailor their investment strategy to match their risk tolerance and long-term goals. If they understand the potential returns and associated risks, they can make choices that align with their financial aspirations.

Example 2 - Personal Finance:

Suppose someone is determined to achieve financial freedom by managing their money wisely. Educating themselves about personal finance concepts, like budgeting and debt management, allows them to take control of their financial trajectory. They may choose to live below their means, pay off high-interest debt, and invest their savings strategically—all of which contribute to long-term wealth accumulation.

TAKING OWNERSHIP OF YOUR FINANCES:

The quote "No one will care about your money more than you do" underscores the importance of being proactive in managing your finances. When you invest time and effort in learning about finance, you take charge of your financial destiny. Instead of relying solely on financial advisors or institutions, you become an active participant in making decisions that impact your wealth.

Example 3 - Empowered Decision-Making:

Imagine an individual who actively learns about investing and decides to manage their own investment portfolio. By understanding the principles of asset allocation and portfolio diversification, they can construct a well-balanced investment strategy. This approach can lead to cost savings by avoiding unnecessary fees and commissions associated with managed funds.

Example 4 - Long-Term Perspective:

Consider someone who educates themselves about the power of compounding. Armed with this knowledge, they start investing early in life and consistently contribute to their investment accounts. Over time, the compounding effect grows their wealth exponentially, allowing them to reach their financial goals faster and with more security.

investing in your financial education is an investment in your future. By staying informed about investment options, financial markets, and personal finance concepts, you gain the tools and confidence needed to make sound financial decisions. Ultimately, your proactive approach to learning empowers you to take control of your financial well-being, paving the way for wealth creation and achieving the sought-after goal of financial freedom.

Real Estate as a Tangible and Durable Asset

Real estate investing offers a powerful avenue to build wealth and secure financial freedom by capitalizing on the potential for property appreciation and rental income. Here's an elaboration on the basics of real estate investment, along with famous quotes that underline key principles:

BASICS OF REAL ESTATE INVESTMENT:

Real estate investment involves purchasing properties with the goal of generating income or realizing appreciation over time. It's a strategy that has been favoured by many successful investors due to its potential for long-term financial growth and diversification.

PROPERTY APPRECIATION AND RENTAL INCOME:

Real estate provides two main avenues for wealth creation: property appreciation and rental income. Over time, real estate properties tend to appreciate in value, which can result in significant capital gains when sold. Additionally, owning rental properties allows you to generate regular income through tenant rent payments.

FAMOUS QUOTES RELATED TO REAL ESTATE INVESTMENT:

"Land appreciates, and building depreciates."

This quote highlights a fundamental principle of real estate investment. The value of land tends to appreciate over time, while the physical structures on the land (buildings) tend to depreciate due to wear and tear. This underscores the importance of understanding the underlying value of the land when evaluating real estate investments.

"The three most important things about real estate is location, location, location."

This famous quote emphasizes the critical role that location plays in real estate investment. The desirability and potential for property appreciation are heavily influenced by the property's location. A well-situated property in a thriving area is more likely to attract tenants and experience value growth.

"Don't wait to buy real estate. Buy real estate and wait."

This quote underscores the concept of long-term investment in real estate. While real estate values may experience fluctuations in the short term, a patient approach to holding onto property can lead to significant appreciation over time.

"The best investment on Earth is Earth."

This quote emphasizes the enduring value of real estate as an investment. Land is a finite resource, and owning a piece of it can offer long-term financial security.

Real estate investment presents a multifaceted opportunity to build wealth and achieve financial freedom through property appreciation and rental income. By understanding the dynamics of property values, the importance of location, and the potential for steady returns, investors can strategically leverage real estate as a powerful asset class in their wealth-building journey.

Learn the Fundamentals of Investing in the Stock Market

Understanding the basics of investing in the stock market is crucial for creating wealth and achieving financial freedom. Here's an elaboration on the statement along with famous quotes that emphasize key principles:

BASICS OF STOCK MARKET INVESTING: LEARNING THE FUNDAMENTALS:

Investing in the stock market offers the potential to grow your wealth over time through ownership of shares in publicly traded companies. However, successful stock market investing requires a solid foundation of knowledge and principles to navigate its complexities effectively.

KEY CONCEPTS IN STOCK MARKET INVESTING:

1. Risk and Patience:

> Quote: "The stock market is a device for transferring money from the impatient to the patient." - Warren Buffett

This quote by Warren Buffett highlights the importance of patience in stock market investing. Impulsive decisions driven by short-term market fluctuations can lead to losses. Patient investors who understand the inherent volatility and maintain a long-term perspective are more likely to succeed.

2. Research and Informed Decisions:

> Quote: "Risk comes from not knowing what you're doing."
>
> - Warren Buffett

Investing in stocks requires thorough research and staying informed about the companies you invest in. Those who dedicate time to understand a company's fundamentals, competitive landscape, and future prospects can make more educated investment decisions.

3. Diversification and Risk Management:

> Quote: "Diversification may preserve wealth, but concentration builds wealth."
>
> - Warren Buffett

Diversification involves spreading investments across different companies and sectors to reduce risk. While diversification helps preserve wealth during market downturns, focusing on a few high-quality investments can lead to substantial wealth accumulation when done carefully.

4. Long-Term Perspective:

> Quote: "In the short run, the market is a voting machine. In the long run, it's a weighing machine."
>
> - Benjamin Graham

Short-term market fluctuations are often driven by emotions and sentiment. However, over the long term, a company's intrinsic value and performance determine its stock's value. A long-term perspective helps investors focus on underlying fundamentals.

In essence, stock market investing is a journey that requires patience, knowledge, and a disciplined approach. By understanding key concepts, conducting thorough research, and embracing a long-term perspective, you can position yourself to make informed decisions that contribute to creating wealth and achieving financial freedom.

Your network is your net worth

The rich understand the value of building strong relationships and networks. They invest time in nurturing connections with other successful individuals, mentors, and industry leaders. These relationships can open doors to new opportunities, partnerships, and collaborations that can significantly impact their financial success

1. Connecting with Success:

Building relationships with fellow achievers allows the exchange of insights and strategies. Associating with those who have walked a similar path provides the opportunity to learn from their successes and challenges. It's akin to standing on the shoulders of giants, leveraging their wisdom to make informed decisions on your own financial journey.

2. Guidance and Mentorship:

Engaging with mentors provides a unique advantage. Learning from someone who has already navigated the complexities of wealth creation and financial freedom is invaluable. These mentors offer guidance, share their knowledge, and provide a roadmap for avoiding common pitfalls, which can significantly accelerate your progress.

3. Access to Opportunities:

Strong networks often open doors to opportunities that might otherwise remain hidden. Whether it's participating in lucrative ventures, joint ventures, or being part of innovative projects, relationships with industry leaders and like-minded peers grant access to avenues that can contribute to financial growth.

4. Collaborations and Partnerships:

Collaborating with others fosters a synergy that can lead to exceptional outcomes. Partnerships formed within a network of trusted individuals often result in shared ventures that pool resources, skills, and ideas. These collaborations can amplify your capacity to seize larger opportunities and navigate challenges effectively.

5. Mutual Support and Inspiration:

Building relationships and networks creates a supportive ecosystem. Surrounding oneself with peers who share your ambitions fuels motivation and keeps you accountable. Success stories within your network serve as inspiration, showing that achieving financial freedom is indeed possible through dedication and strategic planning.

6. Expanding Horizons:

Networking introduces you to diverse perspectives and ideas. Interacting with individuals from various backgrounds and industries widens your understanding of potential opportunities and different ways to create wealth. This broadens your investment and business horizons, allowing you to make informed decisions beyond your immediate expertise.

Successful individuals, especially those who have attained significant wealth and financial freedom understand that wealth creation and financial freedom are not solitary pursuits. Building relationships and networks is akin to building a foundation of collective wisdom, support, and shared goals. These relationships transcend transactional benefits, nurturing a community that collaborates, inspires, and propels each member towards greater financial success. By investing time and effort into developing these relationships, you open doors to opportunities that have the potential to transform your financial trajectory and pave the way towards your ultimate financial goals.

Quote: "Your network is your net worth."

- Porter Gale

Quote: "Alone we can do so little; together we can do so much."

- Helen Keller

Quote: "The fastest way to success is to learn from those who have already achieved it."

- Tony Robbins

Quote: "Surround yourself with people who are going to lift you higher."

- Oprah Winfrey

Quote: "Success is best when it's shared."

- Howard Schultz

Quote: "Your customer doesn't care how much you know until they know how much you care."

- Damon Richards

Quote: "The richest people in the world look for and build networks; everyone else looks for work."

- Robert Kiyosaki

Quote: "Never underestimate the power of networking."

- Porter Gale

Quote: "The value of a man resides in what he gives and not in what he is capable of receiving."

- Albert Einstein

Quote: "Help others achieve their dreams and you will achieve yours."

- Les Brown

Understand Risk and Reward

Assess the risks associated with your investments and balance them with potential rewards.

In the pursuit of creating wealth and achieving financial freedom, understanding the concept of risk and reward is paramount. This principle involves evaluating the potential risks linked to your investment decisions and striking a balance between those risks and the potential rewards they offer. A well-informed approach to risk and reward can guide you towards making prudent financial choices that align with your goals and aspirations.

KEY COMPONENTS OF UNDERSTANDING RISK AND REWARD:

1.   Risk Assessment: Before making any investment, it's essential to thoroughly assess the risks involved. Different investments carry varying degrees of risk, such as market volatility, economic changes, and business-specific challenges. Understanding these risks helps you make informed decisions based on your risk tolerance and financial objectives.

2.   Potential Rewards: Every investment opportunity offers potential rewards, such as capital appreciation, dividends, interest, or rental income. Evaluating these potential rewards helps you gauge the attractiveness of an investment

in terms of its potential to contribute to your financial goals.

3. Risk Tolerance: Your risk tolerance is your ability and willingness to withstand potential losses. It's essential to align your investments with your risk tolerance, as taking on more risk than you can handle emotionally or financially can lead to stress and poor decision-making.

4. Diversification: Diversifying your investment portfolio across different asset classes, industries, and geographical regions is a strategy to manage risk. Diversification can help mitigate the impact of a poor-performing investment on your overall portfolio.

5. Long-Term Perspective: Understanding risk and reward involves adopting a long-term perspective. Short-term market fluctuations might lead to temporary losses, but focusing on the potential rewards over an extended period can lead to more favourable outcomes.

IMPORTANCE OF BALANCING RISK AND REWARD:

1. Minimizing Losses: A balanced approach to risk and reward ensures that you don't expose yourself to excessive losses. By understanding and managing risks, you can protect your capital from significant erosion.

2. Maximizing Returns: While managing risk is crucial, avoiding all risk might result in missed opportunities for growth. Balancing risk and reward allows you to seek investments that offer the potential for higher returns while still aligning with your risk tolerance.

3. Adapting to Circumstances: Economic and market conditions change over time. A balanced approach to risk and reward allows you to adjust your investment strategy

to adapt to evolving circumstances without making hasty decisions driven solely by fear or greed.

EXAMPLE:

Sarah is considering two investment opportunities: investing in a well-established stock with historically stable returns and investing in a startup with high growth potential. While the stock offers lower risk, the startup carries a higher level of risk due to its early-stage nature. Sarah evaluates her risk tolerance, financial goals, and the potential rewards of each investment. Recognizing that she is comfortable with a certain level of risk, she decides to allocate a portion of her portfolio to the startup for the potential of higher returns. However, she also maintains a significant portion in the stable stock to balance her risk exposure.

Understanding risk and reward is a fundamental principle in the journey towards wealth creation and achieving financial freedom. By assessing the risks associated with investments and balancing them with potential rewards, you can make informed decisions that align with your risk tolerance and long-term objectives. This approach empowers you to manage risks effectively while seeking opportunities that contribute to your financial growth and overall financial well-being.

Diversification: Don't put all your eggs in one basket

This principle involves allocating your investments across a variety of asset classes, such as stocks, bonds and real estate, to minimize the impact of poor performance in any one area and enhance the potential for favourable returns. By diversifying wisely, you can build a more resilient and balanced portfolio that aligns with your financial goals.

KEY COMPONENTS OF DIVERSIFICATION:

1. Asset Allocation: Asset allocation is the process of determining how much of your investment capital you allocate to each asset class. Different asset classes have different risk and return profiles. By diversifying your allocations, you reduce the risk of heavy losses in case a particular asset class underperforms.
2. Risk Reduction: Diversification mitigates the impact of market volatility and unexpected events on your portfolio. While some assets may experience downturns, others may remain stable or even appreciate, helping to offset potential losses.
3. Potential for Returns: Different asset classes perform well at different times and under various economic conditions. Diversification ensures that you have exposure to potential

growth opportunities, even if some assets are currently underperforming.

4. Long-Term Stability: Diversification contributes to the stability of your portfolio over the long term. Instead of relying heavily on a single investment, your portfolio's value is less susceptible to drastic fluctuations.

5. Risk Tolerance Consideration: Diversification allows you to tailor your investments to your risk tolerance. If you are risk-averse, you can allocate a larger portion to more stable assets, while still benefiting from exposure to growth assets.

EXAMPLE:

Consider an investor who allocates all their funds to stocks in a single industry. If that industry faces economic challenges, the entire investment could suffer significant losses. However, by diversifying across stocks, bonds, and real estate, the investor spreads their risk. Even if one sector experiences a downturn, the overall impact on the portfolio is minimized, and potential gains from other areas can offset losses.

Diversification is a fundamental principle in the pursuit of creating wealth and achieving financial freedom. By spreading investments across different asset classes, you reduce risk exposure and position your portfolio to benefit from a range of growth opportunities. This approach contributes to the stability and resilience of your investments, aligning with your risk tolerance and long-term financial goals. Diversification is a strategic tool that empowers you to navigate the complexities of the financial markets with greater confidence and increased potential for long-term success.

Keeping a Long-Term Perspective

The best time to plant a tree was 20 years ago. The second-best time is now.

Embracing a long-term perspective in your financial endeavours is akin to planting a tree. The idea is that while starting early is ideal, taking action at any point in time is far more valuable than waiting indefinitely. This principle emphasizes the importance of investing with a long-term horizon in mind, regardless of market conditions, to capitalize on the potential benefits of compounding and navigate market fluctuations.

KEY COMPONENTS OF KEEPING A LONG-TERM PERSPECTIVE:

1. Time as an Ally: Just as a tree grows stronger and taller over the years, your investments have the potential to multiply through compounding. The earlier you start, the more time your investments have to grow and accumulate wealth.

2. Market Fluctuations: Financial markets are prone to short-term ups and downs due to various factors, including economic events and investor sentiment. A long-term perspective allows you to weather these fluctuations and avoid making reactive decisions based on short-term volatility.

3. Power of Compounding: Compounding is the process where your investments generate earnings, and those earnings, in turn, generate more earnings. Over time, the compounding effect can significantly amplify the growth of your investments.

4. Overcoming Procrastination: Waiting for the "perfect" time to start investing often leads to missed opportunities. By taking action now, even if it's not as early as you'd like, you begin the journey toward wealth creation.

IMPORTANCE OF A LONG-TERM PERSPECTIVE IN WEALTH CREATION:

1. Maximized Growth: A long-term approach allows your investments to ride out the market's natural fluctuations and capture the potential for long-term growth. This maximization of growth potential is especially crucial for achieving financial freedom.

2. Consistent Strategy: A long-term perspective encourages you to stick to your investment strategy even during challenging times. Consistency is key to realizing the full benefits of your chosen approach.

3. Reduced Emotional Impact: Short-term market volatility often triggers emotional decision-making. A long-term perspective helps you remain focused on your goals and avoid being swayed by temporary market movements.

EXAMPLE:

Consider two individuals, Alice and Bob. Alice started investing in her 20s, while Bob procrastinated until his 40s. Even though Alice's initial investments were modest, the compounding effect allowed her investments to grow significantly over time. On the other hand, Bob had less time for his investments to compound, even if he contributed more money. This example illustrates that the best time to start investing is early, but starting now is far better than delaying any further.

"Planting the tree" of your financial future by adopting a long-term perspective is an essential principle for creating wealth and achieving financial freedom. Regardless of when you start, committing to a long-term horizon allows you to harness the power of compounding and navigate the challenges of market fluctuations. Remember that the best time to start investing was indeed in the past, but the second-best time is now. By taking action today and maintaining a steadfast focus on your long-term goals, you set yourself on a path towards financial success and the realization of your aspirations.

Learn from Failures

Success is not final; failure is not fatal: It is the courage to continue that counts.

Learning from failures is a fundamental principle in navigating the complex world of investing. Each setback presents an opportunity to refine your strategies, enhance your decision-making, and build a more resilient portfolio

KEY COMPONENTS OF LEARNING FROM FAILURES:

1. Mindset Shift: Instead of viewing failures as setbacks or defeats, adopt a growth-oriented mindset that treats failures as valuable experiences that contribute to your overall financial education.

2. Analysing Mistakes: Each failure provides insights into what went wrong, whether it was a miscalculation, inadequate research, or unforeseen circumstances. Analysing mistakes helps you identify patterns and make informed adjustments.

3. Continuous Improvement: Learning from failures promotes an ongoing cycle of improvement. You refine your investment strategy, mitigate potential pitfalls, and increase your chances of making more successful decisions in the future.

4.   Adaptation: The ability to adapt and evolve based on your experiences is a hallmark of successful investors. Adjust your investment approach by incorporating the lessons learned from failures to enhance your future outcomes.

FEW FAMOUS QUOTES

1.   Quote: "I've missed more than 9000 shots in my career. I've lost almost 300 games. 26 times, I've been trusted to take the game-winning shot and missed. I've failed over and over and over again in my life. And that is why I succeed." - Michael Jordan

Financial Principle: **Embracing failures as part of the learning process helps you adapt and grow, ultimately leading to greater success in your investment journey.**

2.   Quote: "Success is not final, failure is not fatal: It is the courage to continue that counts." - Winston Churchill

Financial Principle: **Viewing failure as a temporary setback encourages resilience and the determination to persist in refining your investment strategy.**

3.   Quote: "I have not failed. I've just found 10,000 ways that won't work." - Thomas Edison

Financial Principle: **Learning from mistakes helps you refine your approach, ultimately leading to more informed and effective investment decisions.**

4. Quote: "Failure should be our teacher, not our undertaker. Failure is delay, not defeat. It is a temporary detour, not a dead-end street." - Denis Waitley

    Financial Principle: **Failure is a stepping stone to growth. Analysing your investment failures allows you to adjust your strategies and redirect your path toward success.**

5. Quote: "The only real mistake is the one from which we learn nothing." - Henry Ford

    Financial Principle: **Extracting lessons from failures ensures that mistakes become valuable opportunities for improvement in your investment approach.**

6. Quote: "You don't learn to walk by following rules. You learn by doing, and by falling over." - Richard Branson

    Financial Principle: **Taking action and being willing to experience failures is essential for gaining valuable insights and expertise in the world of investing.**

7. Quote: "Failure is the condiment that gives success its flavour." - Truman Capote

    Financial Principle: **Embracing failures as part of your journey adds depth and perspective to your investment success, making your achievements all the more rewarding.**

EXAMPLE:

Imagine you invested in a startup that ultimately faced financial difficulties and resulted in a loss. Instead of being disheartened, you could analyse the factors that led to the startup's failure. Perhaps you realized that the company lacked a viable business model, or it faced fierce competition. This analysis prompts you to adjust your investment strategy. In the future, you might focus on startups with clearer value propositions or explore industries with more favourable market dynamics.

Learning from failures is a fundamental principle in the journey towards creating wealth and achieving financial freedom. Embracing failures as opportunities for growth, rather than setbacks, allows you to refine your investment strategy, enhance your decision-making abilities, and develop a resilient mindset. Each failure becomes a stepping stone toward success as you extract valuable lessons and use them to adapt your approach. By incorporating these lessons into your investment journey, you position yourself to make more informed decisions, navigate challenges, and ultimately realize your financial aspirations.

PRINCIPLE 29

Think like an Investor

The secret to investing is to figure out the value of something – and then pay a lot less.

This principle encourages you to adopt a perspective that transcends everyday consumption and focuses on recognizing opportunities within investments. Developing this mindset empowers you to identify potential sources of financial growth, make informed decisions, and take steps that align with your long-term financial goals.

KEY COMPONENTS OF THINKING LIKE AN INVESTOR:

1. **Shift in Perspective:** Thinking like an investor involves shifting your mindset from a passive consumer to an active participant in wealth-building. You start viewing money not just as a means of spending but as a tool for creating more wealth.

2. **Opportunity Recognition:** Instead of seeing expenditures solely as expenses, you begin to recognize opportunities for investments. This might involve investing in assets that can appreciate over time, generate passive income, or contribute to your financial security.

3. **Long-Term Focus:** An investor mindset encourages a focus on the long term. You consider the potential for

financial growth over time rather than seeking instant gratification through impulsive spending.

4. **Analytical Thinking:** Developing an investor mindset means approaching financial decisions with an analytical approach. You assess potential returns, risks, and future implications before making choices.

IMPORTANCE OF THINKING LIKE AN INVESTOR IN WEALTH CREATION:

1. **Wealth Accumulation:** An investor mindset lays the foundation for wealth accumulation by channelling resources into investments that have the potential to appreciate or generate returns over time.

2. **Maximized Financial Potential:** Rather than allowing money to pass through your hands without a purpose, an investor mindset seeks to leverage it for maximum financial potential and growth.

3. **Active Participation:** Thinking like an investor encourages active participation in your financial journey. You become more engaged in your financial decisions and are motivated to make informed choices that contribute to your goals.

EXAMPLE:

Consider two individuals, Alex and Emily. Alex has a consumer mindset, and when he receives a bonus at work, he uses it to purchase luxury items. On the other hand, Emily has developed an investor mindset. When she receives a bonus, she allocates a portion to invest in stocks and puts another portion into a real estate crowdfunding platform. Over time, Emily's investments grow, providing her with additional sources of income and contributing to her wealth creation goals.

Thinking like an investor is a fundamental principle in the journey towards creating wealth and achieving financial freedom. By developing a mindset that recognizes opportunities in investments and the potential for financial growth, you set yourself on a path of active participation, strategic decision-making, and long-term focus. This approach enables you to leverage your financial resources more effectively, make choices aligned with your aspirations, and work towards realizing your dreams of financial stability and freedom.

PRINCIPLE 30

Avoid Emotional Decisions

Keep emotions in check when making financial decisions, as fear and greed can lead to poor choices.

The principle of avoiding emotional decisions stands as a crucial foundation. This principle underscores the significance of maintaining a rational and disciplined approach when making financial choices. By understanding and controlling the emotions of fear and greed, individuals can prevent impulsive actions that might hinder their financial progress.

KEY COMPONENTS OF AVOIDING EMOTIONAL DECISIONS:

1. **Fear and Greed Dynamics:** Fear and greed are powerful emotions that often influence financial decisions. Fear may prompt individuals to sell investments hastily during market downturns, while greed can lead them to chase high-risk opportunities for quick gains.

2. **Rational Decision-Making:** Rational decision-making involves analyzing financial options based on objective information and logical reasoning, rather than being swayed by momentary emotions.

3. **Long-Term Perspective:** Emotional decisions often focus on short-term gains or losses. Keeping a long-term perspective helps individuals make choices aligned with their overarching financial goals.

4. **Discipline and Self-Control:** Developing the discipline to resist emotional impulses and maintain self-control in the face of market fluctuations is essential for effective financial decision-making.

IMPORTANCE OF AVOIDING EMOTIONAL DECISIONS IN WEALTH CREATION:

1. **Mitigated Risk:** Emotional decisions driven by fear and greed can lead to excessive risk-taking or unnecessary losses. By keeping emotions in check, individuals can mitigate risks associated with impulsive actions.
2. **Consistency in Strategy:** An emotionally charged approach might result in frequent changes to investment strategies, hindering the potential for consistent and well-considered growth.
3. **Minimized Regret:** Emotional decisions often lead to regret when short-term outcomes diverge from long-term goals. Rational decision-making helps minimize the potential for such regrets.

EXAMPLE:

Imagine an investor named Sarah who purchased a stock based on a tip from a friend. The stock price initially increased, triggering a sense of greed. However, a market correction caused the stock's value to plummet, leading to fear-driven panic selling. If Sarah had avoided emotional decisions, she might have researched the stock thoroughly, considered its long-term potential, and made a more informed choice.

Avoiding emotional decisions is a fundamental principle in the pursuit of creating wealth and achieving financial freedom. By keeping emotions like fear and greed in check, individuals can make rational, well-informed financial choices that align with their long-term goals. Cultivating the ability to make decisions based on objective analysis rather than fleeting emotions empowers individuals to navigate market fluctuations, maintain consistency in their investment strategies, and ultimately work toward realizing their financial aspirations.

PRINCIPLE 31

Evaluate Return on Investment (ROI)

Assess the returns you expect from an investment compared to the risks involved.

ROI is a fundamental metric used to measure the profitability of an investment by comparing the returns gained to the resources, time, and effort invested. This principle underscores the importance of making informed decisions that consider both potential returns and associated risks, ensuring that your investment choices align with your financial goals.

KEY COMPONENTS OF EVALUATING ROI:

1. **Quantifying Returns:** ROI involves quantifying the financial gains or returns that an investment is expected to generate. This can include factors like capital appreciation, interest, dividends, or rental income, depending on the type of investment.

2. **Understanding Risks:** Evaluating ROI extends beyond just assessing potential gains. It requires a thorough understanding of the risks associated with the investment, including market volatility, economic factors, industry trends, and other variables that could impact the outcome.

3. **Balancing Risk and Reward:** The assessment of ROI involves striking a balance between the potential returns and the level of risk involved. Investments with higher

potential returns often come with greater risks, and investors must weigh these factors to make prudent decisions.

4. **Informed Decision-Making:** ROI assessment requires research, analysis, and due diligence. Making investment choices based on solid information and data reduces the likelihood of making uninformed or impulsive decisions.

IMPORTANCE OF EVALUATING ROI FOR WEALTH CREATION AND FINANCIAL FREEDOM:

1. **Maximizing Returns:** By evaluating ROI, you can identify investments that have the potential to provide higher returns, aligning with your goal of creating wealth and achieving financial freedom.

2. **Risk Mitigation:** Understanding the risks associated with an investment allows you to take measures to mitigate potential losses. Proper risk assessment helps you make choices that protect your capital.

3. **Efficient Resource Allocation:** Evaluating ROI enables you to allocate your resources effectively. It helps you identify investments that provide the best potential returns for the resources you're committing.

4. **Long-Term Planning:** ROI assessment encourages a long-term perspective. Investments with higher ROI potential may require time to realize substantial gains, aligning with the goal of achieving financial freedom over the long term.

EXAMPLE:

Sarah is considering two investment opportunities: investing in a startup with high growth potential and investing in a stable government bond. The startup offers a higher potential ROI due to its innovative nature, but it also carries a higher level of risk.

The government bond, while offering lower returns, is considered a safer investment. To make an informed decision, Sarah assesses the expected ROI of both investments, taking into account her risk tolerance and financial goals. Ultimately, she decides to allocate a portion of her portfolio to the startup for its higher potential returns, but she also maintains a significant portion in the government bond for stability.

Evaluating Return on Investment (ROI) is a cornerstone of sound financial decision-making. By assessing potential returns against associated risks, you can make informed investment choices that align with your goals of creating wealth and achieving financial freedom. This principle emphasizes the importance of considering both quantitative and qualitative factors, enabling you to build a diversified and resilient portfolio that can weather market fluctuations and contribute to your long-term financial success.

Consider Tax Implications

Understand the tax implications of your investments and explore tax-saving options.

Judge Learned Hand who was a former Judge of the United States District Court in early 20th century once said: "Anyone may arrange his affairs so that his taxes shall be as low as possible; he is not bound to choose that pattern which best pays the treasury. There is not even a patriotic duty to increase one's taxes."

1. "Understand the tax implications of your investments..."

Meaning: Every investment you make, whether in stocks, real estate, bonds, or other assets, comes with potential tax consequences. These can significantly affect your returns.

The after-tax return on investments often matters more than the nominal return. Two investments might offer the same return on paper, but if one is taxed more heavily than the other, its real return will be lower. To maximize wealth, investors need to understand and account for these tax implications.

2. "explore tax-saving options."

There are numerous legitimate ways to reduce your tax liability through various tax-saving options. This can be through tax-advantaged investments, tax deductions, credits, or specific investment vehicles designed to offer tax benefits.

Money saved on taxes is money that can be reinvested to generate more wealth. By consistently taking advantage of tax-saving options, you can supercharge your wealth growth over the long term. The compound effect of these savings and the growth they generate can significantly accelerate the journey to financial freedom.

3. "Minimizing tax is legitimate..."

Governments often create tax incentives to promote certain behaviours, like saving for retirement, investing in certain sectors, or buying a home. Taking advantage of these incentives to reduce your tax liability is both legal and wise.

Minimizing taxes isn't just about saving money; it's about aligning your financial behaviour with broader economic or societal goals recognized by the government. Doing so not only saves you money but often leads to other types of financial benefits and can form a solid base for sustainable wealth creation.

4. "avoiding tax is not."

While minimizing taxes within the framework of the law is acceptable, actively hiding income or assets to evade taxes is illegal and unethical.

Tax evasion can lead to severe penalties, including fines and imprisonment. The short-term gains achieved by evading taxes can be wiped out many times over by the consequences of getting caught. Moreover, sustainable wealth creation is built on a foundation of integrity and ethical behaviour. Engaging in illegal activities undermines this foundation and can jeopardize all other wealth-building efforts.

Achieving financial freedom is a long-term journey that requires strategy, discipline, and knowledge. Taxes play a critical role in this journey. By understanding the tax landscape and making informed decisions, investors can navigate the path to wealth more effectively and ethically. Avoiding pitfalls, like tax evasion, and leveraging benefits, like tax incentives, can significantly influence the speed and sustainability of wealth accumulation.

PRINCIPLE 33

Invest in Yourself

Prioritize your personal and professional development to increase your earning potential.

1. **Warren Buffett** - "The best investment you can make is in yourself."
2. **Benjamin Franklin** - "An investment in knowledge always pays the best interest."
3. **Jim Rohn** - "Formal education will make you a living; self-education will make you a fortune."
4. **Malcolm X** - "Education is the passport to the future, for tomorrow belongs to those who prepare for it today."
5. **Brian Tracy** - "Your greatest asset is your earning ability. Your greatest resource is your time."
6. **Robert Kiyosaki** - "The most important investment you can make is in yourself."
7. **Dalai Lama** - "When you talk, you are only repeating what you already know. But if you listen, you may learn something new."
8. **Zig Ziglar** - "If you are not willing to learn, no one can help you. If you are determined to learn, no one can stop you."

These quotes remind us that investing time, effort, and sometimes even money into our own education, well-being, and personal growth can yield some of the highest returns in terms of happiness, success, and financial stability.

Example: Suppose you decide to take a course on digital marketing because you realize it's an in-demand skill. The money and time you invest in that course is an investment in yourself. Once you've gained this knowledge, you might be able to launch a profitable online venture, secure a better-paying job, or offer freelance services, thus directly improving your earning potential.

PRIORITIZE YOUR PERSONAL AND PROFESSIONAL DEVELOPMENT

Development is multi-faceted. While professional development can lead to career advancement and increased earnings, personal development can lead to better decision-making, improved relationships, and overall a better quality of life, which can indirectly influence your financial stability.

Example: On the professional side, imagine you're a software developer. By learning a new programming language or getting a certification, you might position yourself for a promotion or a better job opportunity. On the personal side, by attending workshops on financial literacy, you improve your money management skills, ensuring that you save more, invest wisely, and avoid bad financial decisions.

INCREASE YOUR EARNING POTENTIAL

Earning potential isn't just about the amount you earn today, but what you could earn in the future. By consistently upgrading your skills and knowledge, you stay competitive, open doors to new opportunities, and often command a higher pay or profit.

Example: Consider two graphic designers. Designer A sticks to the skills they know and doesn't keep up with the latest design trends or software. Designer B, on the other hand, regularly attends webinars, learns new software, and understands the evolving market needs. Over time, Designer B might be able to charge clients more due to their advanced skill set, or even land a higher-paying job.

IMPLICATIONS FOR CREATING WEALTH AND ACHIEVING FINANCIAL FREEDOM

1. **Higher Income Streams:** As you enhance your skills and expertise, you can demand a higher salary or charge more for your services. This increased income can be channelled into investments, which over time can compound and contribute to wealth creation.

2. **Diverse Opportunities:** Continuous learning often opens doors to diverse opportunities. Maybe you start with one skill, but as you learn, you might find intersections that lead to new, lucrative ventures.

3. **Future-proofing:** In a rapidly changing world, especially with advancements in AI and technology, continuous self-investment ensures you remain relevant and in-demand.

4. **Improved Decision Making:** Financial freedom isn't just about earning more; it's about managing what you earn wisely. Personal development, especially in areas of financial literacy, ensures you make informed decisions that protect and grow your wealth.

the journey to financial freedom is not just about external investments but also about internal growth. By focusing on personal and professional development, you build a foundation that not only increases your earning potential but also equips you with the tools to manage and multiply your wealth effectively.

Stay Informed

Keep yourself updated on economic trends, global events, and market news that can impact your investments

At its core, staying informed is about empowering oneself with knowledge. In the world of investments, information equates to foresight, enabling one to foresee potential risks and opportunities.

Example: In the late 2000s, those who were well-informed about the U.S. housing market's vulnerabilities and the complex web of financial products tied to it (like mortgage-backed securities) could have potentially mitigated their losses during the 2008 financial crisis, or even profited from it.

ECONOMIC TRENDS

These are broader patterns or phenomena in the economy that can be indicative of future performance. This can include trends like inflation rates, job growth, consumer sentiment, manufacturing output, and more.

Example: If you're informed and recognize early signs of a country heading into a recession (e.g., declining manufacturing orders, rising unemployment), you might adjust your investment portfolio by reducing exposure to assets typically sensitive to economic downturns, like certain stocks, and increasing your position in safer assets like government bonds.

GLOBAL EVENTS

Global events encompass a range of occurrences – from political upheavals and trade wars to pandemics and natural disasters. These events can drastically affect industries, currencies, and entire economies.

Example: During the onset of the COVID-19 pandemic in early 2020, investors who were quick to understand the global ramifications of the virus might have repositioned their portfolios by reducing exposure to sectors like travel and hospitality while increasing positions in sectors such as healthcare, technology, or e-commerce.

MARKET NEWS

Staying updated with market news means being aware of specific events that can affect particular industries or companies. This can include product launches, mergers and acquisitions, earnings reports, regulatory changes, and more.

Example: An informed investor who closely follows tech news would have been aware of Apple's intention to develop its own chip (Apple Silicon) for its Mac computers, potentially reducing their investments in companies previously supplying chips to Apple, anticipating a decrease in sales for those suppliers.

IMPLICATIONS FOR CREATING WEALTH AND ACHIEVING FINANCIAL FREEDOM

1. **Risk Management**: Being informed allows investors to understand and manage risks better. By anticipating

potential pitfalls, one can restructure investments to mitigate possible losses.

2. **Seizing Opportunities**: A well-informed investor can spot opportunities earlier than others, allowing them to enter (or exit) positions advantageously.

3. **Diversification**: Understanding global events and trends can help investors diversify their portfolios effectively. Diversification, or spreading investments across various assets or regions, can protect wealth from localized risks.

4. **Long-term Strategy**: While it's essential to stay updated, it's equally vital not to overreact to short-term news. Knowledge allows investors to differentiate between transient market noise and genuinely impactful events, helping them stick to a long-term strategy without making impulsive decisions.

Staying informed is a keystone habit for anyone serious about building wealth and achieving financial freedom. Knowledge not only illuminates risks and opportunities but also cultivates a mindset of proactive adaptation, ensuring one's financial strategy evolves with the changing landscapes of the world.

Stay Disciplined

Stick to your investment plan and resist impulsive decisions based on short-term market fluctuations.

1. **Warren Buffett** - "The stock market is designed to transfer money from the active to the patient."
2. **Benjamin Graham** - "The investor's chief problem – and even his worst enemy – is likely to be himself."
3. **Peter Lynch** - "You get recessions, you have stock market declines. If you don't understand that's going to happen, then you're not ready, you won't do well in the markets."
4. **Jesse Livermore** - "The game of speculation is the most uniformly fascinating game in the world. But it is not a game for the stupid, the mentally lazy, the person of inferior emotional balance, or the get-rich-quick adventurer. They will die poor."
5. **John Bogle** - "Time is your friend; impulse is your enemy."
6. **Sir John Templeton** - "The four most dangerous words in investing are: 'This time it's different.'"
7. **Paul Samuelson** - "Investing should be more like watching paint dry or watching grass grow. If you want excitement, take $800 and go to Las Vegas."
8. **George Soros** - "It's not whether you're right or wrong that's important, but how much money you make when you're right and how much you lose when you're wrong."

9. **Seth Klarman** - "The single greatest edge an investor can have is a long-term orientation."

10. **Robert Arnott** - "In investing, what is comfortable is rarely profitable."

These quotes encapsulate the idea that discipline, patience, and adherence to a well-thought-out plan, rather than chasing short-term trends or reacting to temporary market fluctuations, are key to achieving long-term investment success. Emotions and impulses can be an investor's worst enemies, leading to hasty decisions that often result in losses. As many of these seasoned investors suggest, sticking to one's principles and strategy, even in the face of market volatility, is paramount.

Example: Imagine two investors, Alice and Bob. Alice frequently reacts to market news, buying or selling stocks based on daily headlines. Bob, on the other hand, has a diversified portfolio and a clear strategy for the next 10 years. Even during a market downturn, he remains disciplined and avoids making impulsive decisions. Over a decade, Bob's portfolio, with its compounded returns, is likely to outperform Alice's, which is susceptible to frequent transaction fees and the pitfalls of emotionally driven decisions.

STICK TO YOUR INVESTMENT PLAN

An investment plan is a roadmap, outlining goals, risk tolerance, and strategies. Having and sticking to this plan ensures you make decisions aligned with your long-term objectives and avoid getting sidetracked by short-term noise.

Example: Consider an investor who, after thorough research, decides to invest in a mix of stocks and bonds targeting a 7% annual return over 20 years. During a particular year, the stock market surges, and many are getting returns of over 20%. Instead of being swayed and reallocating all funds into stocks, the investor sticks to the plan, understanding that markets can be cyclical, and today's boom could be tomorrow's bust.

RESIST IMPULSIVE DECISIONS BASED ON SHORT-TERM MARKET FLUCTUATIONS

Markets are inherently volatile in the short term. Reacting to every rise and fall can not only lead to poor decisions but also to high transaction costs, potentially eroding returns.

Example: In March 2020, due to the global panic caused by the COVID-19 pandemic, stock markets around the world plummeted. An impulsive investor might have sold stocks in a panic, locking in significant losses. A disciplined investor, on the other hand, would recognize such events as inherent market risks and, if their long-term investment thesis remained unchanged, might even see such downturns as buying opportunities. Indeed, those who remained patient saw many markets recover and even reach new highs in the subsequent months.

IMPLICATIONS FOR CREATING WEALTH AND ACHIEVING FINANCIAL FREEDOM

1. **Consistent Growth**: By avoiding the pitfalls of frequent buying and selling, you allow your investments to grow consistently, benefiting from the power of compound returns.
2. **Emotional Equilibrium**: Staying disciplined ensures that you're not swayed by the emotional highs and lows of the market. This emotional balance can prevent costly mistakes.

3. **Cost Efficiency**: Constantly reacting to the market typically results in higher transaction fees, which can eat into your returns over time.

4. **Achieving Long-Term Goals**: Wealth creation is usually a long-term Endeavor. By sticking to a plan, you ensure that you're always moving towards your financial objectives, rather than getting sidetracked by short-term distractions.

In the journey to financial freedom requires a disciplined approach to investment, grounded in research, reason, and a long-term perspective. By committing to a well-constructed plan and resisting the allure of short-term market noise, investors can navigate the tumultuous waters of the financial markets and steer a steady course towards their goals.

PRINCIPLE 36

Learn from Successful Investors

Study the strategies and philosophies of successful investors and apply their insights to your own approach.

The principle of learning from and associating with successful individuals is not just limited to the world of finance; it's a universal tenet that can be applied to various aspects of life, from business to personal development. Here are some quotes that underscore this principle:

1. **Jim Rohn** - "You are the average of the five people you spend the most time with."

2. **Charlie Munger** - "I constantly see people rise in life who are not the smartest, sometimes not even the most diligent, but they are learning machines. They go to bed every night a little wiser than they were when they got up, and boy, does that help, particularly when you have a long run ahead of you."

3. **Robert Kiyosaki** - "If you think I'm smart, you should meet my friends."

4. **Napoleon Hill** (from "Think and Grow Rich") - "Deliberately seek the company of people who influence you to think and act on building the life you desire."

5. **Tony Robbins** - "Who you spend time with is who you become."

6. **Mark Cuban** - "It's not about money or connections — it's the willingness to outwork and outlearn everyone."

7. **Andrew Carnegie** - "It marks a big step in your development when you come to realize that other people can help you do a better job than you could do alone."

8. **John Wooden** - "Whatever you do in life, surround yourself with smart people who'll argue with you."

9. **Steven Spielberg** - "The delicate balance of mentoring someone is not creating them in your own image, but giving them the opportunity to create themselves."

10. **Tim Ferriss** - "You are the average of the five people you associate with most, so do not underestimate the effects of your pessimistic, unambitious, or disorganized friends. If someone isn't making you stronger, they're making you weaker."

These quotes emphasize the significance of associating with successful, positive, and forward-thinking individuals. The idea is that by surrounding oneself with such people, one can gain new perspectives, absorb beneficial habits, and get motivated to aim higher. Success is not just about innate talent or luck; it's also about continuous learning, adaptability, and the company one keeps.

LEARN FROM SUCCESSFUL INVESTORS

To understand the value of this principle, think of investment as a skill, similar to playing an instrument or a sport. Just as an aspiring musician might study the techniques of Mozart or Beethoven, or an up-and-coming basketball player might study the plays of Michael Jordan or LeBron James, an investor can benefit immensely from studying the strategies of those who've achieved success in the realm of finance.

Example 1: An individual interested in value investing might study the methodologies of Warren Buffett or his mentor, Benjamin Graham. They would learn about the principle of "intrinsic value," which involves buying stocks at a price below their fundamental worth and holding them until the market recognizes their true value.

STUDY THE STRATEGIES AND PHILOSOPHIES

Every successful investor has unique strategies, methodologies, and philosophies that they swear by. By studying these, one can glean insights that might not be immediately apparent. Understanding the underlying philosophies can also guide an investor in times of market uncertainty.

Example 2: Ray Dalio, the founder of the world's largest hedge fund, Bridgewater Associates, emphasizes the importance of "radical transparency" and "having the best independent thinkers" working together. By understanding his holistic approach, an investor might realize the importance of diversification and not getting emotionally attached to any single investment.

APPLY THEIR INSIGHTS TO YOUR OWN APPROACH

Once an investor has studied the successful strategies and philosophies of renowned investors, the next step is application. It doesn't mean copying their moves verbatim but integrating the learned principles into one's own unique strategy, tailored to personal risk tolerance and investment goals.

Example 3: After reading about Peter Lynch's investment philosophy of "invest in what you know," an individual might decide to analyse and potentially invest in companies within industries they're familiar with or work in. If someone has expertise in the tech sector, they might use their knowledge to identify promising tech startups or undervalued tech giants.

IMPLICATIONS FOR CREATING WEALTH AND ACHIEVING FINANCIAL FREEDOM

1. **Guided Decision Making**: Instead of navigating the complex world of investments on their own, investors can use the wisdom of proven experts to guide their decisions, thereby potentially increasing their chances of success.

2. **Avoid Common Pitfalls**: By understanding the mistakes and lessons learned by successful investors, one can sidestep many common investing pitfalls, ensuring a smoother path to financial freedom.

3. **Continual Learning and Adaptation**: The world of finance and investment is ever-evolving. By making it a habit to learn from the best in the field, investors can keep their strategies updated, allowing them to adapt to changing market conditions and new investment vehicles.

By consciously studying and learning from the best, an investor not only equips themselves with proven strategies but also fosters a mindset of continual learning and adaptation – essential traits for long-term success in the investment world.

PRINCIPLE 37

Control Investment Costs

Minimize investment expenses, such as management fees and commissions, to improve overall returns.

Every person, whether a novice or a seasoned pro, wants to maximize their returns. However, while most people focus on the performance of their investments, many overlook the costs associated with managing and trading those investments. Over time, these costs can significantly erode an investor's overall returns, particularly when compounded. Hence, controlling investment costs becomes paramount.

BREAKDOWN:

1. **Types of Investment Costs:**
    - ○ **Management Fees**: These are fees that funds charge to cover operational costs. It's common with mutual funds, index funds, and ETFs.
    - ○ **Commissions**: Fees paid to brokers for executing trades.
    - ○ **Load Fees**: Sales charges on mutual funds, either when you buy (front-end load) or sell (back-end load).
    - ○ **Expense Ratios**: Ongoing fees that all funds charge, which is a percentage of your assets in the fund.
    - ○ **Advisory Fees**: Fees paid to financial advisors or robo-advisors for their services.

2. **Impact on Returns**:
   - ○ Even small fees can have a big impact over the long run due to compounding. For instance, a 1% annual fee might seem trivial, but over 30 years, it can eat into a significant portion of your returns.

Example: Imagine you invest $100,000 and earn an average of 7% annually. Without any fees, in 30 years, your investment would grow to approximately $761,000. However, with a 1% annual fee, it would only grow to about $574,000. That's a difference of nearly $187,000 due to a seemingly small fee!

3. **Strategy Implications**:
   - ○ **Passive vs. Active Management**: Passive funds, like index funds, typically have lower fees than actively managed funds. They aim to mirror the market, not beat it. Over time, many actively managed funds don't outperform the market, especially after accounting for their higher fees.
   - ○ **Trade Less**: Every time you trade, you might incur a commission. Frequent trading can quickly accumulate costs, especially in accounts without commission-free trading.
   - ○ **Consider Fee-Free Platforms**: Some platforms offer commission-free trading or a selection of no-transaction-fee mutual funds.
4. **Achieving Financial Freedom**:
   - ○ Minimizing fees can accelerate the journey to financial freedom. More of your money stays invested and compounds over time, rather than going to intermediaries.

Example: If two investors both invest $500 a month for 40 years and get an average return of 7%, but one pays 0.5% in fees while the other pays 1.5%, the first investor will end up with nearly $260,000 more at the end of the period. That's a significant amount when considering financial freedom or retirement.

Controlling investment costs isn't just about penny-pinching; it's about ensuring that the bulk of the returns your investments earn stay in your pocket. Over an investing lifetime, this can mean the difference between an average retirement and an early, comfortable financial independence. By being mindful of fees and making strategic choices, investors can significantly bolster their financial outcomes.

PRINCIPLE 38

Focus on Cash Flow

When investing in rental properties or businesses, prioritize positive cash flow to generate income.

Here are some quotes that encapsulate the importance of focusing on cash flow:

1. **Robert Kiyosaki (author of 'Rich Dad Poor Dad')** - "Cash flow is the most important term in the world of money. The second most important is leverage."
2. **Warren Buffett** - "Our favourite holding period is forever." This quote underscores the importance of investments that consistently generate positive cash flow over the long term.
3. **Michael S. Clouse** - "Profit is not a result; it's a must. Without it, any business will soon be on its deathbed."
4. **Robert Kiyosaki** - "Financial freedom is available to those who learn about it and work for it."
5. **Dave Ramsey** - "You must gain control over your money, or the lack of it will forever control you."
6. **Robert Allen** - "The best investment is in the tools of one's own trade."
7. **Grant Cardone** - "You will never be wealthy if you're not obsessed with getting equity."

These quotes emphasize the importance of not just seeking profit, but also maintaining consistent income (cash flow) from investments. Positive cash flow, especially from assets like rental properties or businesses, allows for both sustenance and growth, forming the bedrock of long-term wealth creation and financial freedom.

At its core, cash flow represents the net amount of cash or cash-equivalents being transferred into and out of a business or property. In the context of creating wealth, positive cash flow indicates that an asset (like a rental property or business) is generating more income than it has in expenses.

WHY IS CASH FLOW IMPORTANT?

1. **Liquidity:** Positive cash flow ensures that there's enough liquidity for both planned expenses and unexpected ones. It's the lifeblood of any business or investment.
2. **Reinvestment:** A strong cash flow allows for reinvestment, which can further enhance the earning potential of an asset.
3. **Debt Management:** Cash flow can help manage and reduce any debts associated with the business or property, thereby reducing interest expenses and increasing overall profitability.
4. **Reduced Dependency:** With consistent positive cash flow, there's less dependency on external financing or selling assets in emergencies.
5. **Valuation:** Assets, especially businesses, are often valued based on their cash flow. Higher consistent cash flow can significantly increase the asset's value.

EXAMPLES:

1. **Rental Properties**: Consider a rental property purchased for investment. If the monthly rental income from tenants is $2,000 and the total expenses (including mortgage, maintenance, taxes, and insurance) amount to $1,500, the net positive cash flow is $500/month or $6,000/year. This consistent income stream can be used to pay down the mortgage faster, save for future property investments, or cover any unexpected repairs.

2. **Businesses**: Let's say someone starts a cafe. After all expenses (salaries, rent, utilities, inventory), if the cafe makes more money than it spends each month, it has a positive cash flow. This extra money can be reinvested to perhaps open a new branch, upgrade equipment, or introduce a new menu to attract more customers.

ACHIEVING FINANCIAL FREEDOM:

1. **Compounding Growth**: Over time, as you reinvest the positive cash flow from one asset, you can acquire additional assets, creating multiple streams of income.
    Example: Using the income from one rental property to put a down payment on another, over time, leads to a portfolio of properties, all generating income.

2. **Financial Buffer**: Positive cash flow acts as a buffer against downturns. If rental demand drops or the business faces a tough month, having a history of strong cash flow provides a cushion.

3. **Income Replacement**: For those aiming for financial freedom, the goal is often to have investment cash flow replace their regular job income.
    Example: If someone requires $5,000 a month to cover all personal expenses and they have rental properties

generating $7,000 a month after expenses, they have essentially achieved a level of financial freedom.

Prioritizing cash flow isn't just about immediate gains; it's about building a sustainable, long-term wealth generation strategy. By ensuring that investments, be it in properties or businesses, consistently produce more income than they consume in expenses, investors can not only grow their wealth but also secure it against potential financial downturns, putting them on a solid path towards financial freedom.

Invest in Low-Cost Index Funds

Consider low-cost index funds for diversified exposure to the stock market.

One of the foundational ways to manage risk is through diversification, or spreading your investments across a wide array of assets. Index funds, especially those that come with low costs, have become a favoured vehicle for achieving such diversification in an efficient manner.

WHAT ARE LOW-COST INDEX FUNDS?

Low-cost index funds are investment funds that track a specific market index, such as the S&P 500, ASX 200 or the Total Stock Market Indexes. They aim to replicate the performance of the index they track, providing broad market exposure. Because they are passively managed (i.e., they simply aim to mirror an index rather than actively picking and choosing stocks), they usually come with much lower fees than actively managed funds.

Investing in low-cost index funds has become a staple piece of advice from many financial experts due to the funds' diversified nature and low fees. Here are some quotes that emphasize this principle or touch upon related ideas:

1. **Warren Buffett** - "A low-cost index fund is the most sensible equity investment for the great majority of investors."

2. **John C. Bogle (founder of Vanguard and pioneer of the index fund)** - "Don't look for the needle in the haystack. Just buy the haystack!"

3. **Burton Malkiel (author of 'A Random Walk Down Wall Street')** - "A blindfolded monkey throwing darts at a newspaper's financial pages could select a portfolio that would do just as well as one carefully selected by experts."

4. **Charlie Munger (Warren Buffett's business partner)** - "The whole idea of the index fund is you just don't believe that anyone can pick stocks that will do better than average, so you just buy them all. It's a very sound idea."

5. **David Swensen (Yale's Chief Investment Officer)** - "Establishing a dominant position in mainstream markets (like by using index funds) proved to be of paramount importance."

These quotes underline the importance of recognizing the benefits of broad market exposure and the cost savings associated with low-cost index funds. Many have come to believe that consistent market timing and stock selection are nearly impossible for the majority of investors. As such, low-cost index funds that aim to mirror the market provide a solid foundation for most portfolios.

EXAMPLES:

1. **S&P 500 Index Fund:** Let's say an investor puts their money into an index fund that tracks the S&P 500, which comprises 500 of the largest publicly traded companies in the U.S. By doing so, they essentially own a small portion of each of those 500 companies. If a few companies in

the index underperform, the strong performance of the other companies can help to offset these losses, stabilizing returns.

2. **International Index Funds**: An investor looking for global exposure might invest in an index fund that tracks a global or international index, allowing them to benefit from growth in various regions of the world without having to pick individual stocks or countries.

3. **Cost Comparison**: Consider two investors, each investing $10,000. One invests in an actively managed fund with a 1.5% annual fee, while the other chooses a low-cost index fund with a 0.05% annual fee. Even if both funds achieve the same gross return of 7% annually, over 30 years, the investor in the index fund could have tens of thousands of dollars more due to the fee difference alone.

For many individuals seeking financial freedom, the ability to invest without needing to become a stock-picking expert is crucial. Low-cost index funds offer a pathway to participate in the stock market's growth, without the need for extensive research or the risks associated with trying to "beat the market." Over time, the compounded returns from these funds, especially given their lower fees, can play a pivotal role in achieving financial independence.

Investing in low-cost index funds provides a straightforward, efficient, and cost-effective means for investors to gain exposure to the stock market. With the benefits of broad diversification and historically competitive returns, these funds have become a staple in the portfolios of those seeking long-term wealth creation and financial freedom.

PRINCIPLE 40

Avoid Timing the Market

Avoid trying to time the market and focus on staying invested for the long term.

The concept of "timing the market" refers to the strategy of buying or selling investments based on predictions of future market movements. It's the idea that you can jump in just before the market goes up and jump out just before it goes down. While this might seem like a sound approach on paper, in practice, it's extremely challenging and often counterproductive.

WHY AVOIDING MARKET TIMING IS CRUCIAL:

1. **Predicting Short-Term Movements is Nearly Impossible**: Financial markets are influenced by a multitude of factors, including economic data, corporate earnings, geopolitical events, and even unexpected global occurrences (e.g., pandemics). Predicting how all these variables will interact at any given moment is virtually impossible.

2. **Missed Opportunities**: Studies have shown that a significant portion of the stock market's gains over time come from just a handful of the best trading days. If an investor is not in the market on these days, their long-term returns can be severely impacted. Attempting to time the

market increases the risk of missing out on these crucial days.

3.   **Increased Costs**: Frequent buying and selling can lead to increased transaction fees and potentially higher capital gains taxes, eroding returns over time.

4.   **Emotional Stress**: Trying to time the market can also lead to unnecessary stress and anxiety, which can, in turn, lead to poor decision-making.

EXAMPLES:

1.   **Dot-Com Bubble**: In the late 1990s, many investors believed that tech stocks were the future and that they would continue to rise indefinitely. When the dot-com bubble burst in 2000, those who had tried to time the market by heavily investing in tech stocks at their peak suffered significant losses. However, investors who maintained a diversified portfolio and held on through the downturn saw their investments recover and grow in the following years.

2.   **2008 Financial Crisis**: Following the housing market crash and subsequent financial crisis in 2008, many investors, fearing a prolonged downturn, sold their stocks. Those who tried to time the market by selling at the bottom missed out on the subsequent bull market that began in March 2009 and ran for over a decade, one of the longest in history.

3.   **A Hypothetical Investor**: Consider two investors, each starting with $10,000. Investor A tries to time the market, hopping in and out based on news and predictions. Investor B simply invests in a diversified mix of stocks and holds for 20 years. If Investor A misses just the best 10 trading days over that 20-year period, their return could be cut in half

(or worse) compared to Investor B, who remained invested the entire time.

For many individuals, financial freedom means having the resources to live life on their own terms without being overly concerned about finances. One of the proven paths to this freedom is consistent, long-term investing. When investors avoid the temptation to time the market and instead commit to a strategy of consistent investing over the long term, they allow their assets the time to compound and grow, which can lead to significant wealth creation.

While the allure of timing the market and securing quick profits can be enticing, history and data suggest that a long-term, disciplined approach to investing is more likely to lead to wealth and financial freedom. By focusing on the long term and resisting the urge to react to short-term market movements, investors can position themselves for greater success and fewer headaches.

HERE ARE SOME QUOTES EMPHASIZING THIS PRINCIPLE:

1. **Peter Lynch (legendary mutual fund manager of Fidelity's Magellan Fund)** - "Far more money has been lost by investors preparing for corrections, or trying to anticipate corrections, than has been lost in corrections themselves."

2. **Sir John Templeton (founder of the Templeton Growth Fund)** - "The four most dangerous words in investing are: 'This time it's different.'"

3. **Jason Zweig (financial journalist)** - "Whenever you're tempted to short the market or make a timing bet, do something else instead. Take a nap. Take a walk. Take a hike. Don't take a risk."

4. **Warren Buffett** - "Our favourite holding period is forever."

5. **Paul Samuelson (Nobel Laureate in economics)** - "Investing should be more like watching paint dry or watching grass grow. If you want excitement, take $1000 and go to the casino."

6. **James W. Michaels (former editor of Forbes magazine)** - "Stop trying to predict the direction of the stock market, the economy or the elections."

7. **Nick Murray** - "Timing the market is a fool's game, whereas time in the market is your greatest natural advantage."

8. **Warren Buffett** - "Nobody buys a farm based on whether they think it's going to rain next year. They buy it because they think it's a good investment over 10 or 20 years."

These quotes emphasize the inherent unpredictability of the investment markets in the short term and the potential perils of trying to capitalize on its fluctuations. Over the long term, however, the market tends to reward those who remain patient and steadfast in their investment approach.

Avoid Get-Rich-Quick Schemes

Beware of schemes promising quick riches and prioritize sustainable wealth-building strategies.

Get-rich-quick (GRQ) schemes are strategies or propositions that promise to generate significant returns on an investment in a very short time. While the allure of rapid wealth is tempting, such schemes often involve substantial risk, deception, or outright fraud.

WHY IT'S CRUCIAL TO AVOID GET-RICH-QUICK SCHEMES:

1. **High Risk**: GRQ schemes often involve speculative investments, which carry high risk and can result in substantial losses.
2. **Lack of Transparency**: Many such schemes are shrouded in secrecy, with promoters providing little clarity on how the returns are generated.
3. **Potential Fraud**: Historically, numerous GRQ schemes have turned out to be scams, where money from new investors is used to pay returns to earlier investors—a classic example of a Ponzi scheme.
4. **Unsustainability**: Even if a scheme is initially profitable, its business model might be unsustainable, leading to eventual collapse.

5. **Emotional Decision Making**: GRQ schemes often play on human emotions like greed, fear of missing out, or desperation, leading individuals to make impulsive and ill-informed decisions.

EXAMPLES:

1. **Ponzi Schemes**: Named after Charles Ponzi, who became infamous in the 1920s, a Ponzi scheme is where returns to earlier investors are paid using the capital of newer investors. The scheme collapses when there aren't enough new investors to pay previous ones. One of the largest and most famous Ponzi schemes was operated by Bernie Madoff, resulting in billions of dollars in losses.

2. **Pump and Dump Stocks**: Promoters inflate the price of a stock by spreading misleading positive news to increase demand. Once the stock price is artificially pumped up, they sell (dump) their shares. When the truth comes out, the stock price crashes, leaving other investors with substantial losses.

3. **Pyramid Schemes**: Participants recruit new participants to pay up-front costs. The returns to the initial promoters are paid using the investments of new participants, and so on. The system eventually collapses under its weight, leaving those at the bottom with losses.

4. **High-Yield Investment Programs (HYIPs)**: These online investments promise incredibly high returns but are often Ponzi schemes in disguise.

5. **Internet Scams**: These include email scams promising vast inheritances in exchange for an upfront fee or investment.

While the idea of becoming instantly wealthy is enticing, real and lasting financial success is usually the result of patience, discipline, and a well-informed strategy. Avoiding get-rich-quick schemes and focusing on proven, sustainable wealth-building methods increases the likelihood of achieving financial freedom and security.

Avoid Investing Based on Tips

Do your own research rather than investing solely based on tips or rumours.

The world of investing is rife with "hot tips" and rumours about the next big stock or lucrative opportunity. While it's tempting to act on such advice, especially if it comes from a seemingly trusted source, making decisions based solely on such tips can be detrimental. Sound investment decisions are rooted in diligent research, understanding of the market, and a clear investment strategy, rather than impulsive reactions to often-unverified information.

REASONS TO AVOID INVESTING BASED SOLELY ON TIPS:

1. **Unreliable Source**: Tips can come from any source - a friend, family member, coworker, or even strangers on the internet. The reliability and intention of the tipster are usually unknown, and they might not have done their own due diligence.

2. **Incomplete Information**: Even if the tip is accurate, it might only provide a partial picture. Investing requires a holistic understanding of the opportunity, including potential risks, which a simple tip cannot provide.

3. **Herding Behaviour**: Acting on rumours can lead to "herding", where investors follow the majority without

proper analysis. This behaviour can inflate stock prices and lead to bubbles that eventually burst.

4. **Emotional Decision Making**: Tips often come with a sense of urgency, leading investors to make hasty, emotion-driven decisions rather than well-thought-out ones.

EXAMPLES DEMONSTRATING THE IMPORTANCE OF RESEARCH:

1. **Dot-Com Bubble**: In the late 1990s and early 2000s, there was a surge in investment in internet-based companies, driven in part by rumours and speculations. Many of these companies didn't have solid business models or earnings to justify their stock prices. Investors who followed the hype without research saw significant losses when the bubble burst.

2. **Cryptocurrency Hype**: While there are legitimate and valuable cryptocurrencies, the market has seen a surge in 'altcoins' of questionable value. Many investors, lured by tips and rumours of the next "Bitcoin," have invested heavily in these lesser-known coins without proper understanding, leading to significant losses when their values plummeted.

3. **Individual Stock Tips**: An individual might hear a tip that a certain company is about to be acquired, leading to a potential surge in stock price. Without verification and understanding the broader context, investing based on this tip can be risky. If the acquisition falls through or was never in the works, the stock might underperform.

THE VALUE OF RESEARCH:

Doing one's own research ensures that an investor is well-informed about the strengths, weaknesses, opportunities, and threats associated with an investment. This research can include studying a company's financial statements, understanding industry trends, and considering geopolitical and macroeconomic factors.

While tips and rumours can sometimes offer valuable insights, they should never be the sole basis for investment decisions. The most successful investors prioritize diligent research and base their choices on a comprehensive understanding of the market and the specific investment opportunity. This approach not only maximizes the potential for gains but also minimizes the risk of significant losses.

Avoid High Credit Card Debt

Pay off high-interest credit card debt as quickly as possible to reduce financial stress.

Credit cards, when used thoughtlessly, can be a double-edged sword. On one hand, they offer convenience, rewards, and can even boost your credit score when used responsibly. On the other, they can lead to mounting debt, high interest payments, and financial stress if not managed correctly.

REASONS TO MINIMIZE OR ELIMINATE HIGH CREDIT CARD DEBT:

1. **High Interest**: Credit cards typically come with much higher interest rates than other types of loans. Carrying a balance on a credit card means you're paying a premium on your purchases.

2. **Compounding Debt**: When you don't pay off your credit card in full, the interest compounds. This means you're paying interest on your past interest, causing the amount you owe to grow exponentially.

3. **Financial Stress**: Debt can be a significant source of stress, affecting mental well-being and leading to other health issues. Constantly worrying about paying off high balances can strain personal relationships and hinder daily life activities.

4. **Credit Score Implications**: High credit card utilization (i.e., using a large portion of your credit limit) can negatively impact your credit score. A lower credit score can result in higher interest rates when taking out loans or even being declined for credit.

STRATEGY: USE CREDIT CARDS WISELY FOR BENEFITS, NOT FOR DEBT

Many financial experts recommend that, instead of avoiding credit cards altogether, you use them to your advantage but always pay off the full balance.

1. **Loyalty Points & Cashback**: For instance, some credit cards offer loyalty points or cashback on purchases, which can lead to savings or benefits if you consistently pay off the balance. For example, if a card offers 2% cash back on all purchases and you spend $2,000 a month on the card (but pay it off in full every month), you could earn $480 in cash back over a year.

2. **Building Credit**: Regular use of a credit card, followed by timely and complete payments, can build a positive credit history. This can be especially important for younger individuals or those trying to rebuild their credit.

3. **Travel Perks**: Some cards offer travel benefits, like free checked bags or access to airport lounges. If you travel frequently, these perks can offer real value. For instance, if you avoid a $30 checked bag fee on four flights a year, that's $120 in savings.

4. **Purchase Protections**: Many credit cards come with benefits like extended warranties, price protection, or insurance for car rentals.

REAL-LIFE EXAMPLE:

Imagine two individuals: **Alex** and **Jordan**.

Alex uses her credit card to make all her monthly purchases, accumulating a balance of $3,000 every month. However, instead of paying it off, she pays the minimum balance and carries the rest, accruing high interest. Over the course of a year, not only does she pay a significant amount in interest, but she also feels constant stress about her growing debt.

Jordan, on the other hand, also spends $3,000 a month on his credit card. But he pays off his balance in full every month. He earns loyalty points on his card, which he redeems for travel, and never pays a cent in interest.

Clearly, Jordan is utilizing his credit card more strategically, reaping the benefits without the drawbacks.

Avoiding high credit card debt is critical to maintaining financial health and progressing towards financial freedom. By treating credit cards as a tool for convenience and rewards rather than a vehicle for borrowing, individuals can navigate the financial world more confidently and strategically.

Consider Long-Term Value

Focus on long-term value when making investment decisions, rather than short-term fluctuations

One of the foundational tenets of intelligent investing is the focus on the intrinsic, or long-term, value of an asset rather than its short-term price movements. This approach can help investors avoid impulsive decisions driven by market volatility, allowing them to build and preserve wealth over time.

REASONS TO PRIORITIZE LONG-TERM VALUE:

1. **Reduce Emotional Decision-Making**: By focusing on the long-term potential of an investment, you can minimize the emotional reactions to short-term market swings, which often lead to buying high and selling low.

2. **Capitalizing on Compound Interest**: Albert Einstein famously dubbed compound interest as the "eighth wonder of the world." By keeping investments for a longer duration, you allow interest to compound on interest, leading to exponential growth.

3. **Avoiding Transaction Costs**: Frequently buying and selling assets can result in significant transaction costs, which can erode potential profits. Long-term investing minimizes these costs.

4. **Benefiting from Economic Cycles**: Economies tend to go through cycles of boom and recession. Long-term investing allows you to ride out these cycles, benefiting from the growth periods and weathering the downturns.

REAL-LIFE EXAMPLES:

1. **Amazon Stock**: An investor who judged Amazon's value by its short-term price fluctuations during its early years might have sold the stock after a downturn. However, those who focused on the company's long-term potential and held onto their shares have seen a phenomenal return on their investment as Amazon grew to be one of the world's most valuable companies.

2. **Real Estate**: Consider an individual who buys a home in a developing neighbourhood. Short-term, there might be market downturns, and the house's value may decrease. However, as the area develops over the decades, the house's long-term value could increase substantially, making the initial investment worthwhile.

3. **Warren Buffett's Approach**: Known for his value investing strategy, Buffett often buys stocks of companies that he believes are undervalued but have strong long-term growth potential. By ignoring short-term market noise and focusing on the inherent value, he has achieved remarkable returns over his investing career.

4. **Dot-Com Bubble**: During the late 1990s, many investors were lured by the skyrocketing values of tech stocks and began investing based on short-term gains, ignoring the long-term viability of many of these companies. When the bubble burst in 2000, many of these companies saw their stock values plummet, leading to significant losses

for those who had not considered the long-term value and sustainability of these companies.

While it's natural to be affected by the daily ups and downs of the market, a shift in focus to the long-term potential and intrinsic value of investments can pave the way for sustained wealth creation. This strategy requires patience, diligence, and often a contrarian mindset, but history has shown that it's a path many successful investors have tread. By emphasizing long-term value over short-term fluctuations, investors are better equipped to weather market volatility and capitalize on genuine growth opportunities.

Learn About Asset Classes

Understand different asset classes like stocks, bonds, real estate, and commodities to diversify your portfolio.

Diversifying one's investments across various asset classes is a foundational strategy in financial planning. This approach aims to spread and minimize risk, as different assets typically respond differently to economic events. Understanding each asset class helps an investor tailor their investment strategy to meet specific financial goals, risk tolerance, and time horizons.

Overview of Main Asset Classes:

1. **Stocks (Equities)**: Represent ownership in a company. They have the potential for high returns but also come with higher volatility. Stocks are typically recommended for longer-term goals due to their potential for growth over time.
    - **Example**: An individual invests in shares of a tech startup. After five years, the startup becomes an industry leader, leading to a significant appreciation in the stock price.

2. **Bonds (Fixed Income)**: These are essentially loans made by an investor to a borrower, often corporate or governmental. They tend to be more stable than stocks but usually offer lower potential returns.

○ **Example**: A retiree invests a portion of their savings in government bonds, providing them with regular interest payments and preserving their capital.

3. **Real Estate**: Investing in property, either directly or via Real Estate Investment Trusts (REITs). Real estate can provide rental income and potential appreciation in property value. It's also a tangible asset and can act as a hedge against inflation.

    ○ **Example**: A young couple buys a second property in a growing urban area. Over the next decade, the area becomes a prime location, leading to both rental income and capital appreciation.

4. **Commodities**: Physical goods like gold, oil, or agricultural products. They can act as a hedge against inflation and diversify a portfolio since they might be less correlated with stocks or bonds.

    ○ **Example**: An investor, foreseeing potential economic instability, invests in gold. As economic conditions deteriorate and other assets decline, gold prices surge.

BENEFITS OF UNDERSTANDING AND DIVERSIFYING ACROSS ASSET CLASSES:

1. **Risk Management**: Different asset classes have different risk profiles. By diversifying investments across various assets, you reduce the risk of a significant loss in any single asset.

2. **Balanced Returns**: While one asset class may underperform, another might outperform, leading to more consistent and stable overall portfolio growth.

3. **Flexibility**: Knowledge of different asset classes allows investors to reallocate and adjust their portfolios based on

changing financial goals, market conditions, or personal circumstances.

REAL-LIFE SCENARIO:

Imagine two friends, **Mia** and **Lucas**.

Mia puts all her savings into stocks of tech companies. While she sees significant growth in the initial years, a tech industry downturn leads to a 40% reduction in her portfolio's value.

Lucas, having learned about various asset classes, diversifies his investments. He allocates 50% to stocks across different sectors, 30% to bonds, 10% to real estate, and 10% to commodities. During the same tech downturn, while his tech stocks decline in value, his bonds remain stable, his real estate investments appreciate, and his gold holdings surge due to economic uncertainty.

As a result, Lucas's portfolio is more resilient to industry-specific downturns, and he achieves more consistent growth over time compared to Mia.

Understanding different asset classes is vital for constructing a diversified and balanced portfolio. It allows investors to capture gains from high-performing assets while being shielded from poor-performing ones. As the adage goes, "Don't put all your eggs in one basket." In the investment world, this means spreading investments across different asset classes to navigate the uncertainties of the financial markets effectively.

Focus on Quality, Not Quantity

Invest in a few high-quality assets rather than spreading your investments too thin.

The principle of focusing on quality over quantity in investments suggests that it's better to hold a concentrated portfolio of excellent assets than a diversified portfolio of mediocre ones. By emphasizing the quality of investments, an investor ensures that each asset in their portfolio holds strong potential for growth and sustainability.

BENEFITS OF FOCUSING ON QUALITY:

1. **Stronger Return Potential**: High-quality assets, whether stocks, real estate, or other investments, tend to possess intrinsic values that can lead to higher returns over time. They often have a track record of performance, solid fundamentals, and a competitive edge in their respective markets.

2. **Reduced Risk**: While diversification is a strategy to manage risk, investing in high-quality assets is another. Quality investments tend to be more resilient during economic downturns and volatile market conditions.

3. **Simplified Portfolio Management**: Managing a smaller number of investments allows for deeper understanding and tracking of each asset. It becomes easier to stay updated on relevant news and make informed decisions.

REAL-LIFE EXAMPLES:

1. **Blue-Chip Stocks**: An investor who chooses to invest in blue-chip companies, like Apple or Microsoft, is focusing on quality. These companies have a history of stable earnings, strong balance sheets, and often pay dividends. Even though these stocks may face short-term fluctuations, their long-term growth potential is considered stable due to their market leadership and financial strength.

2. **Prime Real Estate**: Instead of buying multiple properties in lesser-known areas, an investor might choose to buy a single property in a prime location known for its appreciation potential. Over time, this prime property might yield better returns due to its location, even if the initial investment was higher.

3. **Warren Buffett's Approach**: The legendary investor Warren Buffett is known for his focus on quality over quantity. He often says, "It's far better to buy a wonderful company at a fair price than a fair company at a wonderful price." His investments in companies like Coca-Cola and American Express are testaments to this approach. Instead of diversifying into hundreds of stocks, he has historically held a more concentrated portfolio of companies he believes have excellent long-term prospects.

COUNTERPOINT:

While focusing on quality is crucial, it's essential to understand the risks of a concentrated portfolio. Without adequate diversification, if one of the few high-quality assets underperforms or faces an unforeseen issue, it can significantly impact the overall portfolio's value. Hence, it's a balance between ensuring quality and managing risk through diversification.

The emphasis on quality over quantity is about making each investment count. It's about ensuring that every dollar invested has the best chance of growing over time. By carefully selecting high-quality assets after thorough research and analysis, an investor positions themselves for sustainable wealth creation. However, it's equally crucial to be aware of the risks and ensure that there's a strategy in place to manage potential downturns.

Avoid Emotional Trading

Stay disciplined and avoid making investment decisions based on fear or greed.

Emotional trading refers to making investment decisions based on strong emotions, such as fear, greed, or even pride, rather than on solid research, analysis, and a well-defined investment strategy. Emotional reactions can cloud judgment and lead to impulsive decisions that deviate from one's original investment plan. By staying disciplined, investors can ensure that their choices align with their long-term objectives and risk tolerance.

CONSEQUENCES OF EMOTIONAL TRADING:

1.   **Buying High, Selling Low**: An investor who gets caught up in the excitement of a rapidly rising market (greed) might buy assets at peak prices. Conversely, fear can lead to panic-selling assets during market downturns, often at a loss.

2.   **Overtrading**: Emotional reactions can lead to frequent buying and selling, incurring higher transaction costs and potentially reducing overall returns.

3.   **Missing out on Long-term Growth**: Investors who react emotionally might miss out on the long-term growth potential of certain assets. For instance, selling stocks during a temporary downturn may prevent the investor

from benefiting from potential rebounds and long-term appreciation.

REAL-LIFE EXAMPLES:

1. **2008 Financial Crisis**: During the 2007-2008 financial crisis, many investors, driven by fear, sold their stocks and other assets, incurring heavy losses. Those who remained disciplined and held onto their investments or even bought more during the downturn often saw substantial gains as markets rebounded in subsequent years.

2. **Tech Bubble of the Early 2000s**: The late 1990s and early 2000s saw a surge in technology stocks, fuelled by enthusiasm (greed) for the burgeoning internet sector. Many investors, captivated by soaring stock prices, bought in at elevated levels. When the bubble burst, those who had purchased based on emotion faced significant losses.

3. **Bitcoin and Cryptocurrency Volatility**: Cryptocurrencies like Bitcoin have seen dramatic price swings. Some investors, driven by stories of massive gains (greed), buy in during peaks, only to sell in panic (fear) during sharp declines, locking in losses.

STRATEGIES TO AVOID EMOTIONAL TRADING:

1. **Have a Clear Investment Plan**: Before investing, have a clear understanding of your goals, time horizon, and risk tolerance. This plan will serve as a guideline and prevent knee-jerk reactions to market volatility.

2. **Dollar-Cost Averaging**: This strategy involves investing a fixed dollar amount at regular intervals, regardless of market conditions. It reduces the temptation to time the

market and can lower the average cost of purchasing an asset over time.

3. **Educate Yourself**: Understanding market history and the cyclical nature of investments can provide context during turbulent times, reducing the likelihood of emotional reactions.

4. **Seek Professional Advice**: Financial advisors or investment professionals can provide an objective perspective, helping investors stick to their strategies during emotional times.

Emotions are a natural part of the human experience, but when it comes to investing, they can be detrimental. Staying disciplined and adhering to a well-thought-out investment strategy can mitigate the potential pitfalls of emotional trading. It ensures that decisions are rooted in sound financial principles rather than fleeting feelings, leading to a more consistent path toward wealth creation and financial freedom.

Avoid FOMO

Don't invest out of fear of missing out (FOMO) on a hot investment trend.

FOMO, or the fear of missing out, is an increasingly common sentiment in the age of real-time information and social media. It represents the anxiety that an exciting or interesting event may currently be happening elsewhere, often aroused by seeing posts on social media. In the context of investing, FOMO can manifest as the fear of missing out on the next big investment opportunity or trend. However, making hasty investment decisions based on FOMO rather than solid research and a coherent strategy can be detrimental to one's financial health.

CONSEQUENCES OF INVESTING BASED ON FOMO:

1. **Lack of Due Diligence**: FOMO-driven decisions can lead to skipping crucial research steps, resulting in uninformed investment choices.

2. **Overpaying for Assets**: Jumping into an investment trend during its peak can result in buying assets at inflated prices, increasing the risk of losses.

3. **Heightened Emotional Stress**: FOMO can lead to a roller-coaster of emotions, with investors constantly on edge about "the next big thing" and whether they're missing out.

REAL-LIFE EXAMPLES:

1. **Cryptocurrency Frenzy**: Many individuals, hearing stories of early Bitcoin investors becoming millionaires, invested large amounts at its peak, only to see its value decrease shortly after, leading to significant losses.

2. **Dot-Com Bubble**: In the late 1990s, there was a rush to invest in any company associated with the internet, driven largely by FOMO. Many of these companies failed, leading to substantial losses for those who had invested without adequate research.

3. **Initial Public Offerings (IPOs)**: There's often a lot of hype surrounding IPOs. Investors, fearing they'll miss out on the next big stock, may buy without adequately understanding the company's fundamentals. This can lead to buying at a peak price and potential losses if the stock's value drops post-IPO.

COUNTERING FOMO:

1. **Recognize the Sales Tactic**: As pointed out, FOMO is a tactic used by salespeople and marketers to create urgency. By understanding this, investors can approach opportunities with a more critical mindset.

2. **Always Do Your Research**: Before making any investment, thorough research is crucial. This provides a buffer against impulsive decisions.

3. **Stick to Your Investment Plan**: Having a clear investment strategy helps in resisting the allure of every new trend or "hot tip."

4. **Seek Objective Advice**: Talking to financial advisors or trusted peers can offer a more grounded perspective, away from the frenzy of the market.

While it's natural to feel a sense of urgency when faced with potential opportunities, it's essential to remember that the world of investing is vast. As rightly mentioned, there are always new investment opportunities around the corner. It's more beneficial in the long run to wait for opportunities that align with one's investment strategy, risk tolerance, and research rather than jumping into investments solely due to FOMO. **Sustainable wealth creation is a journey, not a race.**

Focus on Long-Term Sustainability

Invest in companies and industries with a focus on long-term sustainability and ethical practices.

The concept of focusing on long-term sustainability emphasizes the importance of considering the future impact and longevity of your investments. As awareness around environmental, social, and governance (ESG) factors grows, investors increasingly prioritize sustainable and ethical investments. These investments often prioritize not just immediate profit but also the broader societal, environmental, and corporate governance implications of their activities.

ADVANTAGES OF SUSTAINABLE INVESTING:

1. **Risk Mitigation**: Companies that prioritize sustainable practices often have lower risks related to environmental damage, regulatory fines, and social backlash.

2. **Potential for Steady Returns**: Sustainable businesses are often positioned better to handle market disruptions, resource scarcities, and changing regulatory landscapes.

3. **Positive Societal Impact**: Investing in such businesses allows individuals to contribute positively to societal issues like climate change, fair labour practices, and corporate governance.

REAL-LIFE EXAMPLES:

1. **Renewable Energy Companies**: As the world shifts away from fossil fuels, companies in the renewable energy sector, such as those focused on solar or wind energy, present sustainable investment opportunities. Their long-term outlook is strengthened by increasing global awareness of climate change and supportive governmental policies.

2. **Ethical Supply Chains**: Companies like Patagonia emphasize responsible sourcing of materials and fair labour practices. By doing so, they not only ensure ethical operations but also appeal to a growing consumer base concerned with ethical consumption.

3. **Water Preservation Initiatives**: Companies focusing on water-saving technologies or wastewater management offer solutions to the global challenge of water scarcity, positioning themselves as vital players in a sustainable future.

CONSIDERATIONS FOR INVESTORS:

1. **Due Diligence**: Like any investment, it's essential to do thorough research. Some companies may engage in "greenwashing," where they exaggerate their sustainability efforts for marketing purposes.

2. **Diversification**: While investing in sustainable companies, it's still essential to diversify investments across sectors and regions to mitigate risks.

3. **Stay Updated**: The landscape of sustainable industries evolves rapidly. As an investor, staying updated on technological advancements, regulatory changes, and market trends can provide a competitive edge.

The emphasis on long-term sustainability and ethical practices in investing is not merely a trend but a reflection of global shifts in consumer behaviour, regulatory environments, and societal values. By integrating these considerations into investment decisions, investors can align their financial goals with their personal values, ensuring that their wealth grows hand-in-hand with positive societal impact. Investing in this manner not only has the potential for strong financial returns but also fosters a more sustainable and equitable world.

Understand the Power of Saving

Saving money is the foundation of wealth-building; make it a priority.

At its core, the practice of saving money is about discipline, patience, and understanding the concept of delayed gratification. While the immediate returns of saving might seem negligible, especially when compared to potentially lucrative investment opportunities, the act of saving provides a secure foundation upon which wealth can be built. This is achieved through consistent accumulation and the benefits of compound interest over time.

ADVANTAGES OF SAVING:

1. **Safety Net**: Having savings provides a financial buffer during unforeseen circumstances such as medical emergencies, job loss, or unexpected major expenses.

2. **Financial Independence**: A consistent savings habit can lead to significant wealth accumulation over time, granting individuals the freedom to make choices without monetary constraints.

3. **Compound Interest**: Money saved in interest-bearing accounts can grow exponentially over time. Even if the interest rate seems low, over extended periods, the effects of compounding can be substantial.

REAL-LIFE EXAMPLES:

1. **Emergency Fund**: Jane, a young professional, decided to save 10% of her monthly income in an emergency fund. After a few years, when she faced unexpected medical expenses, she was able to cover them without going into debt, all thanks to her foresight and saving habit.

2. **Retirement Savings**: Robert started saving a portion of his income in a retirement account from the age of 25. By the time he reached 65, due to the power of compound interest, he had amassed a sum large enough to retire comfortably without relying on external support.

3. **Down Payment for a Home**: Aisha prioritized saving money from her early twenties. A decade later, she had saved enough to make a significant down payment on a house, reducing her mortgage rate and tenure.

STRATEGIES FOR EFFECTIVE SAVING:

1. **Automate Savings**: By setting up automatic transfers to a savings account, individuals can ensure they consistently save before spending on non-essential items.

2. **Budgeting**: Creating and sticking to a budget helps in distinguishing between needs and wants, making it easier to set aside a portion of income for savings.

3. **Limiting High-Interest Debt**: By avoiding or quickly paying off high-interest debt, especially from credit cards, individuals can save the money that would otherwise go toward interest payments.

While high-return investments are often spotlighted in discussions about wealth-building, the importance of saving should not be underestimated. It provides both a financial safety net and the seed money for future investments. Wealth creation isn't solely about earning high returns; it's equally about preserving and accumulating wealth through disciplined saving. In the journey towards financial freedom, saving is the steady and reliable companion that ensures both stability and growth.

PRINCIPLE 51

Stay Invested During Downturns

Resist the temptation to sell during market downturns; focus on the long term.

Market volatility is an inherent aspect of investing. Prices of assets, especially equities, can swing dramatically in short periods. Many investors, particularly those new to the market, may panic during these downturns and sell their assets to prevent further losses. However, history has shown that markets tend to recover over time. Selling during a downturn often results in realizing losses, while staying invested can offer the potential for recovery and future gains.

Advantages of Staying Invested:

1. **Potential for Recovery**: Historically, after significant downturns, markets have tended to rebound, sometimes reaching new highs.
2. **Benefit from Compound Growth**: Even during downturns, dividends and interest can continue to accrue. Reinvesting these can compound growth over time.
3. **Avoid Timing the Market**: It's challenging to predict market bottoms and tops consistently. By staying invested, you avoid the risk of missing out on sudden market rebounds.

REAL-LIFE EXAMPLES:

1. **2008 Financial Crisis**: Investors who sold their stock holdings during the height of the crisis in 2008-2009 would have missed out on the subsequent decade-long bull market. Those who held onto or even bought more of their investments during the downturn would have seen significant returns as markets recovered and surged to new highs.

2. **Dot-com Bubble**: Post the burst of the dot-com bubble around the year 2000, many tech stocks plummeted. However, those who held onto shares in quality tech companies, like Amazon or Apple, despite short-term losses, have since realized exponential gains.

3. **COVID-19 Market Crash**: In early 2020, global markets experienced rapid declines due to the unforeseen COVID-19 pandemic. Yet, by the end of the year, many markets and individual stocks had not only recovered but reached new highs. Investors who panicked and sold in March would have missed out on this swift rebound.

STRATEGIES FOR STAYING INVESTED:

1. **Diversification**: Having a diverse portfolio spread across different asset classes can mitigate risks and reduce the temptation to sell during downturns in any particular sector.

2. **Regular Rebalancing**: By regularly adjusting your portfolio to maintain desired asset allocations, you can take emotions out of the equation and potentially benefit from buying low and selling high.

3. **Long-Term Perspective**: Always remember your long-term investment goals. Short-term market movements should be viewed in the context of these broader objectives.

While the natural instinct during market downturns may be to protect capital by selling off investments, history suggests that a long-term, patient approach often yields better results. Emotions can be a significant adversary in the investment world. By maintaining a long-term perspective and resisting the impulse to make hasty decisions during market downturns, investors stand a better chance of achieving their financial goals and attaining financial freedom.

Avoid Overextending Borrowing

Be cautious about borrowing too much money to invest, as it can amplify losses.

Borrowing money to invest, often referred to as using leverage or margin, can magnify both potential gains and potential losses. While the allure of using borrowed funds stems from the idea of achieving greater returns on capital, it also brings along the risk of exacerbating losses, which can result in significant financial setbacks or even bankruptcy in extreme cases.

RISKS OF OVEREXTENDING BORROWING:

1. **Magnified Losses**: Just as leverage can increase the potential returns on an investment, it can also amplify losses. If an investor borrows heavily to invest and the investment goes south, they'll not only lose their own money but will also have to repay the borrowed funds.

2. **Margin Calls**: When borrowing to invest in the stock market, a significant drop in the portfolio's value can trigger a margin call. This is a demand by the broker for the investor to deposit additional funds. If the investor cannot meet the margin call, the broker can liquidate the investor's assets at a loss to recover the funds.

3. **Increased Costs**: Borrowing money isn't free. Interest payments on borrowed funds can erode investment returns, especially if the investments underperform.

REAL-LIFE EXAMPLES:

1. **Housing Market Collapse**: Prior to the 2008 financial crisis, many individuals borrowed heavily to invest in real estate, anticipating that property values would continue to rise indefinitely. However, when the housing bubble burst, property values plummeted, leaving many with mortgages far exceeding the value of their properties. This led to widespread foreclosures and was a significant contributor to the global financial meltdown.

2. **Stock Market Margin Calls**: An investor borrows funds to purchase shares of a company they believe will rise in price. However, if the stock's price falls significantly, the broker might issue a margin call, forcing the investor to either deposit more money or sell assets to cover the deficit.

3. **Business Ventures**: Entrepreneurs sometimes borrow heavily to start or expand a business. If the business doesn't perform as expected, they can find themselves in a challenging position, unable to repay the borrowed funds and, in some cases, facing bankruptcy.

STRATEGIES TO MITIGATE BORROWING RISKS:

1. **Conservative Leverage**: If choosing to use leverage, do so conservatively. It's crucial to assess your risk tolerance and not borrow to the extent that potential losses would be catastrophic.

2. **Diversification**: If you're borrowing to invest, ensure your investments are diversified to spread and mitigate potential risks.

3. **Regular Monitoring**: Frequently monitor and assess the performance of leveraged investments. Be prepared to take corrective actions if things start moving in an undesired direction.

While borrowing to invest can be tempting, especially in rising markets, it's crucial to understand the associated risks. Overextending borrowing can lead to severe financial consequences. Successful investors and entrepreneurs often exercise caution and are wary of becoming overly leveraged. The principle of "not risking more than you can afford to lose" is particularly relevant when considering borrowing to invest.

PRINCIPLE 53

Regularly Review Investment Strategy

Review your investment strategy periodically to ensure it aligns with your goals.

Your investment strategy isn't something that you set and forget. As life progresses, your personal circumstances, risk tolerance, and financial goals might change. It's vital to ensure your investments are still poised to help you achieve your desired outcomes, especially as new milestones are reached.

IMPORTANCE OF REVIEWING INVESTMENT STRATEGY:

1. **Shifting Financial Goals**: At different stages in life, your financial objectives will change. For instance, in your 20s, you might focus on accumulating wealth and may have a higher risk tolerance. In your 30s and 40s, with the responsibilities of a family, you might shift towards a more balanced approach. As you approach retirement, preservation of capital might become a priority.

2. **Changing Risk Tolerance**: Major life events, like getting married, having children, or nearing retirement, can affect how much financial risk you're willing or able to take. As these events occur, adjusting your investment strategy can ensure it aligns with your current comfort level.

3. **Market Dynamics**: The financial market isn't static. Economic conditions, interest rates, and geopolitical events

can influence market performance. Periodic reviews can help you adjust your strategy to current market conditions.

REAL-LIFE EXAMPLES:

1. **Starting a Family**: Let's say you started investing in high-risk stocks in your late 20s. Now, in your mid-30s, you have two children and a mortgage. The need for financial security might push you to diversify your portfolio by adding more stable assets, like bonds or real estate.

2. **Approaching Retirement**: Imagine you're in your late 50s, and most of your investments are in equities. As you approach retirement, you might want to reduce exposure to market volatility. Shifting some assets into bonds or fixed-income securities could be a prudent move.

3. **Economic Recession**: If an economic downturn hits and your portfolio is heavily invested in sectors sensitive to recessions, you might decide to reallocate funds to more recession-proof areas or defensive stocks.

4. **New Investment Opportunities**: During your periodic review, you might come across new investment vehicles or sectors that weren't on your radar before, like cryptocurrency or green energy stocks. Depending on your risk tolerance and goals, you might decide to allocate a portion of your portfolio to these new opportunities.

Life is dynamic, and so are financial markets. Regularly reviewing and adjusting your investment strategy can help you stay on track to achieve your financial goals. This is especially crucial when major life changes occur. A strategy that worked for a single individual might not be suitable for someone with a growing family. By taking time to review and adjust, you're actively working towards ensuring your investments serve your current needs and future ambitions.

PRINCIPLE 54

Consider Dollar-Cost Averaging

Dollar-cost averaging helps mitigate the impact of market volatility on your investments.

Dollar-cost averaging (DCA) is a strategic approach where an individual invests a fixed dollar amount in a particular investment at regular intervals, regardless of the asset's price. By doing so, over time, they buy more units when prices are low and fewer units when prices are high, potentially reducing the overall average cost per share of the investment.

ADVANTAGES OF DOLLAR-COST AVERAGING:

1. **Mitigating the Impact of Volatility**: DCA ensures that an investor is not trying to time the market or make lump-sum investments at inopportune times. This reduces the potential negative impact of buying at market highs.
2. **Reduces Emotional Investing**: DCA helps keep emotions out of investment decisions. Rather than trying to guess the best time to buy or sell, you stick to a consistent investment plan.
3. **Financial Discipline**: By committing to regular contributions, investors instil a habit of saving and investing, which can positively influence wealth accumulation over time.

REAL-LIFE EXAMPLES:

1. **Consistent Monthly Investments**: Imagine Sarah decides to invest $100 every month into a stock mutual fund. Over the course of a volatile year:
    - ○ In January, the fund price is $50, so she buys 2 shares.
    - ○ In February, the fund price drops to $25, so she buys 4 shares.
    - ○ In March, the fund price rises to $33.33, so she buys 3 shares.

    By the end of March, Sarah has spent $300 and owns 9 shares, averaging a cost of $33.33 per share. If she had invested the entire $300 in January, she would have only 6 shares. Thanks to DCA, Sarah bought more shares when prices were low.

2. **Retirement Accounts**: Many individuals use DCA with their workplace retirement accounts. Every pay check, a consistent amount is invested in their chosen funds, regardless of market conditions.

3. **Volatile Markets**: Consider John, who started investing just before a market downturn. If he had invested a lump sum, his initial investment would have significantly decreased in value. However, by using DCA, John continued to invest throughout the downturn, purchasing more shares at lower prices. When the market eventually recovered, John benefited not only from the upswing but also from the additional shares he had acquired at lower prices.

Dollar-cost averaging is a methodical approach that can shield investors from the unpredictability and short-term fluctuations of the market. It's particularly beneficial for those who might be hesitant about investing a large amount at once or are unsure about market timing. By spreading out investments over time, DCA can provide a level of protection against the volatility inherent in financial markets and promote disciplined, consistent investing.

Avoid Chasing Hot Stocks

Resist the urge to chase after hot stocks or trends; focus on long-term value.

The allure of "hot stocks" or the latest market trends can be tantalizing for many investors. These are often companies or sectors that have experienced rapid growth in a short period, leading to significant media coverage and hype. While they might offer substantial returns in a short timeframe, they often come with higher risks. The key is to differentiate between short-term noise and long-term value.

RISKS OF CHASING HOT STOCKS:

1. **Increased Volatility**: Hot stocks or sectors tend to be more volatile. This means that the price can swing dramatically in both directions in a short period.
2. **Timing Issues**: It's challenging to time the market correctly. By the time a stock is recognized as "hot," it might already be nearing its peak.
3. **Potential Overvaluation**: Due to the hype and increased demand, these stocks might be overpriced. When the market corrects such overvaluations, late investors can face substantial losses.

ADVANTAGES OF FOCUSING ON LONG-TERM VALUE:

1. **Stable Returns**: Stocks with a strong foundation and growth potential often provide more stable and consistent returns.

2. **Reduced Emotional Stress**: Investing in fundamentally sound stocks means you're less likely to be swayed by market noise and daily fluctuations.

3. **Compounding**: Long-term investments allow the principle of compounding to work in your favour. The returns generated on your investments themselves become part of the investment, leading to potentially higher growth over time.

REAL-LIFE EXAMPLES:

1. **Tech Bubble of the Late 1990s**: Many investors were lured into buying stocks of internet companies (often without clear business models or earnings) because they were rising rapidly. However, when the bubble burst, these stocks plummeted, leading to significant losses for those who had chased the trend without considering fundamentals.

2. **Consistent Growth Stocks**: Consider companies like Microsoft or Johnson & Johnson. While they might not have the allure of the latest tech start-up, their consistent growth and strong fundamentals have rewarded long-term investors with stable returns over the years.

3. **GameStop Mania**: In early 2021, GameStop stock experienced an unprecedented surge due to a short squeeze, driven in part by a retail investor frenzy. Many who chased the stock at its peak faced significant losses when it eventually corrected.

While the allure of hot stocks can be strong, especially when stories of rapid gains circulate, it's crucial to approach investing with a clear strategy. A focus on long-term value, company fundamentals, and sustainable growth is more likely to lead to stable wealth accumulation. Investing should be viewed as a marathon, not a sprint. Avoiding the siren call of trendy stocks and maintaining a disciplined approach is often the key to long-term financial success.

Avoid herd mentality

Do your own research and avoid following the crowd in investing

This is a phenomenon in which individuals make decisions based on what a large group of people are doing, rather than on their own analysis or instinct. In financial markets, this often translates to buying assets when everyone else is buying (and prices are high) and selling when everyone else is selling (and prices are low).

1. BENEFITS OF AVOIDING HERD MENTALITY:

1. **Better Decision Making**: Relying on your own research ensures that your investment decisions are based on facts, figures, and your own understanding of the situation.
2. **Potential for Higher Returns**: Going against the grain can often lead to uncovering undervalued investment opportunities.
3. **Risk Management**: When you've done your own research, you're often better prepared to assess the risks associated with an investment.

2. EXAMPLES:

- **Tech Bubble of the late 1990s**: Many investors, driven by the euphoria around tech stocks and influenced by the actions of the majority, poured money into dot-com companies without solid business models or profitability. Those who avoided the herd, did their own research, and were sceptical of the unsustainable valuations protected their wealth when the bubble eventually burst.

- **2008 Housing Crash**: Leading up to 2008, there was widespread belief that housing prices could only go up. Many investors jumped on the bandwagon, buying properties they couldn't afford with the assumption they could sell them at a higher price or refinance later. Those who did their own research recognized the signs of a housing bubble and avoided significant losses when the market collapsed.

- **Cryptocurrency Frenzy**: While the long-term verdict on cryptocurrencies is still out, there have been several instances where extreme price volatility was driven by herd behaviour. Investors who've done their research might recognize when a particular cryptocurrency is overhyped and avoid buying at inflated prices or, conversely, might identify long-term value where others see only short-term hype.

3. ACHIEVING FINANCIAL FREEDOM:

Financial freedom is achieved not just by making sound investment decisions, but also by preserving wealth. By avoiding herd mentality, you not only position yourself to potentially earn higher returns but also protect yourself from the severe losses that can come from getting caught up in financial bubbles or other market irrationalities.

While it's tempting to follow the crowd, especially when it seems like everyone else is making money, history has shown that the majority can often be wrong, especially during times of extreme optimism or pessimism. The key to long-term financial success and freedom is to stay informed, do your own research, and make decisions based on your own convictions and risk tolerance.

Build credit responsibly

Establish a good credit score for future borrowing opportunities.

Building credit responsibly means cultivating a credit history that reflects timely repayments, prudent management of debt, and making wise financial decisions. A good credit score is a testament to these habits and can significantly impact your financial journey, especially when it comes to borrowing money for significant milestones in life.

IMPORTANCE:

1. **Lower Interest Rates**: A strong credit score generally qualifies you for lower interest rates on loans and credit cards. Over the lifespan of a large loan, like a mortgage, even a small reduction in the interest rate can result in significant savings.

2. **Better Loan Approvals**: Lenders are more inclined to approve loans for those with a robust credit history. A good credit score signals to lenders that you're a low-risk borrower, increasing your chances of loan approval.

3. **Negotiation Power**: A high credit score can offer leverage to negotiate a lower interest rate on a new loan or credit card.

4. **More Favourable Terms**: Some financial products, like premium credit cards or special loan types, may only be available to those with the best credit scores.

5. **Rental & Employment Opportunities**: Landlords often check credit scores to gauge whether a potential tenant will be reliable in paying rent. Similarly, some employers check credit scores, particularly for roles that involve financial responsibilities.

EXAMPLES:

1. **Home Purchase**: Consider two individuals, Alex and Jamie. Both want to buy homes priced at $600,000. Alex, having built credit responsibly, secures a mortgage with a 4% interest rate, while Jamie, with a lower credit score, gets a 6% rate. Over a 30-year term, Alex will pay tens of thousands less than Jamie in interest alone, all because of a difference in credit scores.

2. **Starting a Business**: Maria has a dream of opening her own cafe. She has savings but needs a loan to cover the full start-up costs. Because she has always been responsible with her credit, she easily secures a business loan with favourable terms, allowing her to launch her cafe and begin her entrepreneurial journey.

3. **Emergencies**: Life is unpredictable. Leo faces an unexpected medical emergency. Fortunately, due to his excellent credit score, he can open a credit card with a 0% introductory APR, allowing him to manage the unexpected costs without incurring heavy interest.

Building credit responsibly isn't just about getting a loan or a credit card. It's about creating financial security and flexibility for yourself, ensuring that when life's significant moments or unexpected challenges arise, you're well-positioned to handle them. Achieving financial freedom is as much about being prepared for opportunities as it is about managing challenges, and a strong credit score supports both.

Reinvest dividends

Let dividends grow by reinvesting them into more shares or investments.

The concept of reinvesting dividends revolves around the idea of using dividend payments—money received from investments such as stocks or mutual funds—as an additional means of investment rather than as immediate income. By channelling these payments back into buying more shares or investments, an investor sets in motion a cycle of increasing returns, thanks to the magic of compounding.

IMPORTANCE:

1. **Compound Growth**: Reinvesting dividends results in compound growth. With compound growth, you earn returns not only on your principal amount but also on the dividends and previous earnings. This means that growth is exponential over the long term, significantly amplifying your returns.

2. **Increasing Holdings**: When dividends are reinvested, they are used to buy more shares or units of the investment. Over time, this steadily increases the total number of shares or units an investor holds, leading to larger dividend payouts in the future.

3. **Maximizing Returns**: Dividend reinvestment, especially in downturns or flat markets, ensures that an investor

is maximizing potential returns. This is because during such periods, reinvested dividends often buy more shares at lower prices, setting the stage for greater gains during market recoveries.

EXAMPLES:

1. **Steady Growth Stock**: Let's consider Jake, who owns 1000 shares in a company that pays an annual dividend of $2 per share. Instead of taking the $2000 as cash, he chooses to reinvest. If the stock price is $50, he'll acquire an additional 40 shares this year. The next year, his dividends are calculated not just on the original 1000 shares, but on 1040 shares. Over time, this increase compounds, leading to a significantly larger shareholding and dividend receipt than if he had merely taken the dividend as cash.

2. **Dividend Reinvestment Plans (DRIPs)**: Emily is invested in a company that offers a DRIP, allowing dividends to be directly reinvested to purchase more shares, sometimes even at a discount. Over 20 years, she finds that her share count has grown substantially, even though she hasn't invested more of her own money.

3. **Mutual Fund Compounding**: Michael invests in a mutual fund with a solid track record of paying dividends. He opts to reinvest these dividends in purchasing more units of the mutual fund. Over a decade, not only has the value of his units appreciated, but the number of units he possesses has also grown, thanks to the reinvested dividends. This dual growth significantly boosts his total returns compared to if he'd taken the dividends as cash.

Here are some famous quotes that resonate with this principle:

1. **Albert Einstein**
   - **Quote**: "Compound interest is the eighth wonder of the world. He who understands it, earns it; he who doesn't, pays it."
   - **Implication**: Reinvesting dividends is an application of compound interest. By doing so, you earn interest on your interest, which amplifies growth over time.

2. **Warren Buffett**
   - **Quote**: "My wealth has come from a combination of living in America, some lucky genes, and compound interest."
   - **Implication**: Buffett, one of the most successful investors ever, often speaks about the importance of compound growth. Reinvesting dividends is a method to harness this power.

3. **John D. Rockefeller**
   - **Quote**: "Do you know the only thing that gives me pleasure? It's to see my dividends coming in."
   - **Implication**: While Rockefeller took pleasure in seeing his dividends, modern investors can take it a step further by reinvesting those dividends for future growth.

4. **Benjamin Graham**
   - **Quote**: "The individual investor should act consistently as an investor and not as a speculator."
   - **Implication**: Speculators might chase short-term gains, but true investors think long-term. Reinvesting dividends is a long-term strategy that solidifies an investor's commitment to growth over time.

Reinvesting dividends is akin to planting a seed and then using its fruits to plant even more trees. By consistently reinvesting, an investor not only grows their investment portfolio but also leverages the power of compounding to supercharge their returns. This disciplined approach is a tried and tested path to creating substantial wealth and achieving financial freedom in the long run.

Entrepreneurial mindset

Be open to business opportunities and entrepreneurship.

The entrepreneurial mindset is not just about starting businesses; it's a way of thinking that embraces change, seeks opportunities in challenges, and is not afraid to take calculated risks. This mindset is proactive, innovative, and adaptable, making it a powerful approach for those aiming to create wealth and achieve financial freedom. By being open to business opportunities and cultivating an entrepreneurial spirit, individuals can harness the immense potential of the ever-evolving market landscape.

IMPORTANCE:

1. **Opportunity Recognition**: One of the core components of an entrepreneurial mindset is the ability to spot and capitalize on opportunities. Where others see challenges, entrepreneurs see potential.

2. **Risk Management**: Entrepreneurs are not reckless; they are calculated risk-takers. They evaluate scenarios, weigh the pros and cons, and take steps that they believe will lead to the highest probability of success.

3. **Innovation**: At its core, entrepreneurship is about providing solutions. This often requires thinking outside the box, pioneering new methods, and being willing to adapt.

4. **Resilience**: The path to success is rarely linear. Entrepreneurs expect setbacks but view them as learning experiences, not failures.

EXAMPLES:

1. **Spotting Trends**: Sarah noticed the increasing popularity of eco-friendly products in her community. Instead of just being a consumer, she decided to start a business selling sustainable home goods online. Her proactive approach, in line with market trends, led to a successful venture and significant wealth accumulation.

2. **Pivot and Adapt**: Tom started a business offering guided city tours. However, when the pandemic hit, tourism plummeted. Instead of giving up, Tom adapted by offering virtual city tours, tapping into a market of people eager for travel experiences from the safety of their homes.

3. **Solving Problems**: Aisha lived in a bustling city where finding parking was a constant hassle. She developed an app connecting private parking space owners with drivers in need of a spot. Her solution-oriented approach led to a successful startup and substantial financial gains.

4. **Embracing Failure**: David launched a tech startup which, despite initial promise, didn't gain traction and had to be shut down. Instead of viewing it as a failure, he treated it as a learning experience. He took those lessons and applied them to his next venture, which became a massive success.

Here are some famous quotes that emphasize these principles:

1. **Steve Jobs**
    ○ **Quote**: "Innovation distinguishes between a leader and a follower."

   ○   **Implication**: Embracing an entrepreneurial mindset means being at the forefront of innovation, which is often the key to success in business and wealth creation.

2. **Richard Branson**
   - ○ **Quote**: "Business opportunities are like buses, there's always another one coming."
   - ○ **Implication**: Always be open and ready for the next opportunity. Having an entrepreneurial mindset means being alert to potential ventures and not being disheartened by missed chances.

3. **Oprah Winfrey**
   - ○ **Quote**: "Passion is energy. Feel the power that comes from focusing on what excites you."
   - ○ **Implication**: An entrepreneurial spirit is fueled by passion. Those who find and focus on what they're passionate about often find success and financial growth.

4. **Robert Kiyosaki**
   - ○ **Quote**: "The size of your success is measured by the strength of your desire; the size of your dream; and how you handle disappointment along the way."
   - ○ **Implication**: The journey of entrepreneurship is filled with highs and lows. Maintaining resilience and ambition is crucial for long-term wealth and freedom.

5. **Reid Hoffman (Co-founder of LinkedIn)**
   - ○ **Quote**: "An entrepreneur is someone who jumps off a cliff and builds a plane on the way down."
   - ○ **Implication**: Entrepreneurship is about taking risks and being resourceful. This kind of adaptability can lead to substantial financial rewards.

An entrepreneurial mindset is a potent tool in the quest for wealth creation and financial freedom. It involves more than just starting a business; it's about recognizing opportunities, being resilient in the face of challenges, innovating continuously, and never settling. By embracing this mindset, individuals are better equipped to navigate the complex financial landscape, seize opportunities, and build lasting wealth.

Keep a financial journal

Track your financial progress and learn from your experiences.

Maintaining a financial journal can be likened to a ship's captain keeping a detailed log during a voyage. This logbook doesn't just record the ship's coordinates but also notes the weather conditions, crew morale, equipment status, and more. It is an essential tool for navigation, reflection, and informed decision-making. Similarly, a financial journal acts as a compass in the tumultuous sea of personal finance, providing direction and clarity.

IMPORTANCE:

1. **Accountability and Discipline**: Recording every financial transaction, whether it's income, expenditure, or investment, forces an individual to be accountable. It inculcates discipline in spending and saving behaviours.

2. **Data-driven Decision Making**: Over time, the journal offers tangible data about one's financial habits, enabling data-driven decisions rather than impulsive ones.

3. **Identifying Patterns**: Regular tracking can help identify detrimental financial habits or highlight beneficial ones. This insight can be invaluable in reshaping financial behaviours.

4.   **Goal Setting and Tracking**: A financial journal can serve as a platform to set financial goals and monitor progress toward achieving them.

5.   **Emotional Reflection**: Money is not just a transactional entity; it's deeply intertwined with our emotions. By recording feelings associated with certain financial decisions, one can gain emotional intelligence related to money.

EXAMPLES:

1.   **Identifying Excessive Expenditures**: Let's say John regularly writes in his financial journal. Over a few months, he notices that a significant chunk of his income goes towards dining out. Recognizing this pattern, John decides to allocate a specific budget for eating out and aims to cook more meals at home.

2.   **Investment Tracking**: Maria, an avid investor, uses her journal to track the performance of her stocks. When she reviews her journal at the end of the year, she realizes that a particular stock hasn't been performing well consistently. Based on this data, she decides to re-evaluate her investment in that stock.

3.   **Emotional Purchases**: After a particularly stressful month, Alex realizes, through his journal entries, that he tends to make impulsive purchases when stressed. Recognizing this emotional spending trigger, Alex decides to implement other stress-relieving techniques that don't involve spending money.

4.   **Savings Milestones**: Priya has a goal to save for a down payment on a house. She uses her financial journal to track her monthly savings and celebrate milestones, keeping her motivated and focused on her goal.

Here are some quotes that touch upon the principles related to tracking and learning from financial progress:

1. **Peter Drucker**
   - **Quote**: "What gets measured gets managed."
   - **Implication**: By diligently recording and tracking your financial progress, you become more equipped to manage and improve your financial situation.

2. **Robert Kiyosaki**
   - **Quote**: "It's not how much money you make, but how much money you keep, how hard it works for you, and how many generations you keep it for."
   - **Implication**: A financial journal helps in not just tracking income but also expenses, investments, and long-term financial planning.

3. **Warren Buffett**
   - **Quote**: "The rearview mirror is always clearer than the windshield."
   - **Implication**: Reflecting on past financial entries in your journal can offer clearer insights into your financial habits and decisions than trying to predict the uncertain future.

A financial journal is more than just a record of numbers; it's a reflection of one's financial journey, complete with successes, failures, patterns, and lessons. For those intent on building wealth and achieving financial freedom, a financial journal acts as a guide, teacher, and mirror, shedding light on the path ahead. By learning from past experiences and using that knowledge to inform future decisions, one is better equipped to navigate the complexities of personal finance.

Get adequate Insurance coverage

Have adequate insurance to protect yourself and your assets.

The principle of insurance rests on risk mitigation. Life, in its unpredictability, can present various challenges that can jeopardize one's financial health. Adequate insurance coverage acts as a protective shield, safeguarding not just one's current wealth but also the trajectory of future financial growth. It is the cornerstone of a well-rounded financial strategy.

IMPORTANCE:

1. **Financial Stability**: Unexpected incidents can result in significant expenses. Insurance ensures that such events don't destabilize your financial position.
2. **Peace of Mind**: Knowing that you and your assets are protected allows for peace of mind, enabling you to focus on wealth creation without the constant fear of potential financial setbacks.
3. **Asset Protection**: Assets, whether they're physical (like a home) or intangible (like your ability to earn), are crucial to financial freedom. Insurance ensures that the value of these assets is preserved against unforeseen damages or losses.
4. **Leveraging Opportunities**: Sometimes, to avail certain financial opportunities or to enter business ventures,

having specific insurance coverage is mandated. This ensures you don't miss out on potential wealth-creating ventures.

EXAMPLES:

1. **Health Insurance**: Maria recently had an unexpected health emergency resulting in surgery. Instead of depleting her savings to cover the medical bills, her health insurance took care of the majority of the costs, preserving her path to financial freedom.

2. **Home Insurance**: Alex's house, which was his most significant asset, got damaged in a natural calamity. Thankfully, his home insurance covered the repair costs, preventing a massive dent in his net worth.

3. **Auto Insurance**: Maya was involved in a car accident that wasn't her fault. Her car, a major tool for her business, was severely damaged. Her comprehensive auto insurance took care of the repair costs, ensuring her business operations weren't affected for long.

4. **Disability Insurance**: Ravi, a software developer, suffered a hand injury which made him unable to work for six months. Disability insurance covered a portion of his income during this period, ensuring his financial commitments were met.

5. **Liability Insurance**: Business owner Sam was sued by a customer for an injury that happened in his store. The potential settlement could have bankrupted his business. However, his liability insurance stepped in, covering the legal costs and settlement, thus saving his business.

Here are some quotes from renowned figures and general wisdom that resonate with the principle of safeguarding assets and well-being through insurance:

1. **Benjamin Franklin**
   - **Quote**: "An ounce of prevention is worth a pound of cure."
   - **Implication**: While Franklin was not directly referring to insurance, the sentiment is relevant. Paying for insurance (prevention) can save substantial costs (cure) in case of unforeseen events.

2. **Dave Ramsey**
   - **Quote**: "Insurance transfers risk for events that could sink you."
   - **Implication**: Proper insurance coverage acts as a safety net, protecting you from events that could have catastrophic financial implications.

3. **General Wisdom**
   - **Quote**: "Hope for the best, but prepare for the worst."
   - **Implication**: Insurance is the embodiment of this sentiment, providing a preparation mechanism for the unpredictable challenges life might throw our way.

4. **Anonymous**
   - **Quote**: "Don't insure everything. Just the things you can't afford to lose."
   - **Implication**: It's crucial to prioritize and ensure that you're covered for significant risks and potential high-impact losses.

5. **Robert Kiyosaki**
   - **Quote**: "It's not how much money you make, but how much money you keep, how hard it works for you, and how many generations you keep it for."

○ **Implication**: While this doesn't directly address insurance, the essence is about safeguarding and growing wealth. Insurance plays a pivotal role in ensuring that unexpected events don't deplete what you've worked hard to accumulate.

The journey to wealth creation and financial freedom is not just about increasing income and investments; it's equally about guarding against unforeseen setbacks. While insurance might feel like an overhead cost, especially when one goes years without a claim, its value becomes immeasurable when adversity strikes. Having adequate insurance coverage ensures that the path to financial freedom remains clear, and the milestones set on this journey remain undisturbed.

Start a side hustle

Explore additional income opportunities outside your main job.

In today's dynamic economic environment, relying solely on one stream of income, like a 9-to-5 job, can be limiting in terms of wealth creation and financial security. Starting a side hustle can serve as a strategic approach to diversify income sources, tap into untapped potential, and lay a robust foundation for financial independence. It's about taking control of one's financial destiny and not being overly reliant on a single employer or industry.

IMPORTANCE:

1. **Diversification of Income**: Relying on just one source of income can be risky. An economic downturn, industry shifts, or unexpected job loss can be financially devastating. Having a side hustle provides a safety net, ensuring continuity of income even in uncertain times.

2. **Financial Growth**: Side hustles can significantly boost overall earnings. Over time, what starts as a small side income can grow to match or even surpass primary job earnings.

3. **Skill Development**: Managing a side hustle can help in developing a diverse set of skills – from sales and marketing to finance and operations. These skills can be beneficial in one's primary job or future ventures.

4. **Passion Projects**: Many side hustles begin as passion projects. They offer a platform to pursue personal interests and transform hobbies into income-generating ventures.

Here are some principles in the form of quotes from renowned individuals that reflect the essence of having an additional income stream:

1. **Warren Buffett**
   - ○ **Quote**: "Never depend on a single income. Make investment to create a second source."
   - ○ **Implication**: Diversifying income streams can provide financial stability and

2. **Robert Kiyosaki**
   - ○ **Quote**: "Don't be addicted to money. Work to learn. Don't work for money. Work for knowledge."
   - ○ **Implication**: Side hustles provide a platform not only for additional income but also for learning and skill acquisition, which can be invaluable assets in wealth creation.

3. **Jim Rohn**
   - ○ **Quote**: "Formal education will make you a living; self-education will make you a fortune."
   - ○ **Implication**: Side hustles often involve self-driven learning and innovation. This kind of self-education can lead to unexpected and substantial financial gains.

4. **Anonymous**
   - ○ **Quote**: "Don't wait for opportunity. Create it."
   - ○ **Implication**: A side hustle is often born from recognizing or creating opportunities rather than waiting for them to present themselves.

EXAMPLES:

1. **Freelancing**: Imagine Sarah, a software developer with a tech firm. In her free time, she takes on freelance projects, coding websites for local businesses. Not only does this earn her extra income, but it also helps her hone her skills and build a diverse portfolio.

2. **Online Tutoring**: Raj, a high school math teacher, spends a few hours every weekend tutoring students online. This not only augments his salary but also gives him a sense of accomplishment as he helps students worldwide.

3. **E-commerce**: Mia has always been passionate about handmade crafts. She decides to open an online store on platforms like Etsy, selling her creations. Over time, her hobby transforms into a substantial income source, with customers from around the world.

4. **Real Estate**: Jake works in advertising but has always been keen on the real estate market. He starts by renting out a part of his house on Airbnb. Encouraged by the response, he invests in another property specifically for renting purposes. This side hustle becomes a significant revenue stream and a stepping stone into the world of real estate investments.

5. **Blogging & Affiliate Marketing**: Alex loves traveling and starts a travel blog, sharing his experiences. As his readership grows, he ventures into affiliate marketing, partnering with travel agencies and gear companies. This side hustle not only funds his travels but also becomes a primary income source over time.

Starting a side hustle is more than just about making extra money; it's a strategic move towards financial freedom. By diversifying income streams, one is better positioned to navigate economic uncertainties, seize opportunities, and accelerate the journey to financial independence. Whether it's to pay off debts, save for the future, or invest in passions, a side hustle can be the catalyst propelling individuals closer to their financial goals.

Avoid impulse buying

Practice delayed gratification and think before making purchases.

Financial well-being and the journey towards wealth often depend as much on discipline and restraint as they do on strategic investments and hard work. At its core, impulse buying reflects the human tendency to prioritize immediate pleasure over long-term benefits, often at the detriment of our financial health.

IMPORTANCE:

1. **Financial Discipline**: Avoiding impulse buys is an essential element of financial discipline. It helps ensure that our spending is in line with our financial goals and that we're not squandering resources on non-essential items.

2. **Long-Term Savings**: Money spent impulsively is money that could have been saved or invested. Over time, the cumulative effect of regular impulse purchases can result in significant potential savings or investment gains lost.

3. **Debt Avoidance**: Often, impulse purchases, especially big-ticket items, can lead to accumulating debt, particularly if they are charged to credit cards and not paid off promptly. Avoiding such buys can help keep debt levels manageable.

EXAMPLES:

1. **Tech Gadgets**: Jake, an avid tech enthusiast, is tempted to buy the latest smartphone model, even though his current phone works perfectly fine. If he resists the urge and sticks with his current phone for another year, he could save around $1000 or more, which, if invested, could yield dividends or appreciate in value.

2. **Fashion Sales**: Lucy sees a 50% off sale on a luxury brand. Even though she doesn't need a new handbag, the discount tempts her. By practicing delayed gratification, she could divert that money into her retirement fund or an investment that grows over time.

3. **Online Shopping**: Rahul finds himself browsing e-commerce platforms during his free time, often ending up buying items he hadn't planned for. By setting a rule to wait 24-48 hours before finalizing any online purchase, he allows himself time to reconsider the necessity of the buy, often realizing he doesn't need it.

4. **Grocery Shopping**: Emma shops for groceries when she's hungry, leading her to buy snacks and items that weren't on her list. If she shops after meals and sticks to her list, she could save a significant amount annually.

5. **Cars and Big Purchases**: Daniel wants a car and is enamoured by a high-end model. However, by evaluating his actual needs and considering a slightly older or less luxurious model, he could save thousands of dollars that could be channelled into investments.

Here are some notable quotes and principles from famous individuals that touch on this sentiment:

1. **Warren Buffett**
   - **Quote**: "If you buy things you don't need, you will soon sell things you need."
   - **Implication**: Impulse buying can quickly erode savings and even necessitate the selling of valuable assets. Always ensure your purchases align with your needs and long-term goals.

2. **Dave Ramsey**
   - **Quote**: "We buy things we don't need with money we don't have to impress people we don't like."
   - **Implication**: Many impulse buys are driven by societal pressures or perceived status. Recognize and challenge these motivations to make more intentional financial choices.

3. **Robert Kiyosaki**
   - **Quote**: "If you can't control your emotions, you can't control your money."
   - **Implication**: Impulse buying often stems from emotional triggers. Developing emotional intelligence and self-control can lead to better financial decisions.

4. **Suze Orman**
   - **Quote**: "Just because you can afford it doesn't mean you should buy it."
   - **Implication**: Financial discipline isn't just about managing when money is tight. Even when you have the funds, practicing restraint can lead to better wealth accumulation.

Avoiding impulse buying and practicing delayed gratification are foundational principles for anyone looking to achieve financial freedom. By cultivating habits of intentional spending, individuals can ensure that every dollar spent aligns with their financial goals, paving the way for a future where they are not just financially stable but thriving. It's not just about saving money, but also about channelling funds into avenues that provide long-term growth and stability.

Set financial milestones

Celebrate your financial achievements and set new goals.

The journey to financial freedom is often long and requires persistence. To maintain motivation and keep the path clear, setting tangible financial milestones is imperative. Just as a traveller might mark progress on a map, financial milestones offer markers of your financial journey's progression. They give you something to strive for in the short-term while keeping the long-term vision intact. Celebrating these milestones keeps morale high and offers an opportunity to recalibrate and set new targets.

IMPORTANCE:

1. **Motivation**: Achieving small milestones can provide the motivation needed to tackle larger financial challenges and goals.

2. **Tracking Progress**: Milestones offer a mechanism to monitor how far you've come and how far you still need to go, ensuring you're on the right track.

3. **Adjustment Opportunity**: Celebrating a milestone can also be a time to evaluate and possibly adjust your financial strategies based on what has been learned or any changes in circumstances.

4. **Boosting Morale**: Recognizing and celebrating achievements, no matter how small, can boost morale and

confidence, fostering a positive mindset crucial for wealth creation.

EXAMPLES:

1. **Debt Reduction**: Sarah has a student loan of $50,000. Instead of getting overwhelmed by the large number, she breaks it down and sets a milestone to pay off $10,000 each year. Every time she achieves this annual goal, she treats herself to a small vacation. This not only keeps her motivated but also gives her a break to rejuvenate.

2. **Savings Goal**: Alex aims to buy a house without taking a mortgage. He sets milestones for every $20,000 saved. For each milestone reached, he indulges in a hobby or buys something he's wanted for a while, ensuring he feels the tangible benefits of his discipline and hard work.

3. **Investment Returns**: Priya is new to investing. She starts with a goal to achieve a 5% return on her portfolio. When she achieves that, she celebrates by attending an investment seminar to further her knowledge, setting her next milestone at a 10% return.

4. **Retirement Fund**: Carlos wants to retire with $1 million in his retirement fund. He sets milestones for every $100,000. Each time he hits a milestone, he spends a weekend away with his family, celebrating the journey and building memories.

5. **Side Hustle Income**: Naomi starts a side business. She sets a milestone for the first $1,000 she earns, then $5,000, and so on. For each achieved milestone, she reinvests some of the money back into her business and takes a part to enjoy herself.

Here are some famous quotes and principles that touch on this sentiment:

1. **Tony Robbins**
   - ○ **Quote**: "Setting goals is the first step in turning the invisible into the visible."
   - ○ **Implication**: By creating financial milestones, you're providing a tangible vision for your future financial self, making your dreams actionable.

2. **Dave Ramsey**
   - ○ **Quote**: "A goal without a plan is just a dream."
   - ○ **Implication**: It's not enough to set financial milestones; a structured plan is crucial to bring these milestones to fruition.

3. **Napoleon Hill**
   - ○ **Quote**: "A goal is a dream with a deadline."
   - ○ **Implication**: Financial milestones give a timeframe to your ambitions, making you accountable and providing motivation.

4. **Brian Tracy**
   - ○ **Quote**: "An average person with average talent, ambition and education, can outstrip the most brilliant genius in our society, if that person has clear, focused goals."
   - ○ **Implication**: Consistent efforts toward achieving well-defined financial milestones can lead to remarkable success, even if one doesn't start with abundant resources.

5. **Peter Drucker**
   - ○ **Quote**: "The best way to predict the future is to create it."

○ **Implication**: By setting and working towards financial milestones, you are actively shaping your financial future.

Setting and celebrating financial milestones turns the daunting journey of achieving financial freedom into a series of achievable steps. It allows individuals to feel a sense of accomplishment regularly, which is crucial for maintaining the drive and discipline required for wealth creation. The process not only ensures that financial goals are met but also that the journey is appreciated and enjoyed. Through well-defined milestones, individuals can create a roadmap to financial success, celebrating the small victories along the way and constantly setting sights on new horizons.

Learn from mistakes

Embrace failures as learning opportunities in your financial journey.

The path to financial freedom is not always a straight upward trajectory. It's marked by highs, lows, successes, and failures. However, what differentiates those who ultimately achieve their financial goals from those who don't is often their ability to learn from mistakes. Viewing failures as stepping stones rather than setbacks can significantly transform one's financial journey.

IMPORTANCE:

1. **Personal Growth**: Mistakes are essential for personal growth. They provide clarity, teach resilience, and offer a perspective that success sometimes cannot. By analyzing errors, one can develop a deeper understanding of financial strategies and principles.

2. **Risk Management**: Learning from financial mistakes can enhance your ability to evaluate and manage risks. The more you understand about where things went wrong, the better equipped you are to anticipate future challenges and navigate them.

3. **Decision Making**: Reflecting on past mistakes can sharpen decision-making skills. It encourages an analytical approach, prompting individuals to consider multiple facets of a situation before acting.

4. **Building Resilience**: Embracing failures and moving forward builds resilience, a crucial trait for long-term financial success. Resilience fosters the ability to bounce back from setbacks stronger than before.

EXAMPLES:

1. **Investment Losses**: John invested heavily in a tech startup, drawn by the hype and potential for high returns. Unfortunately, the company didn't perform well, and he suffered significant losses. Instead of being disheartened, John analyzed what went wrong. He realized he'd failed to diversify his investments. Learning from this, John began to diversify his portfolio, spreading his risks and eventually recouping his losses over time.

2. **Neglecting an Emergency Fund**: Priya always believed she had a stable job until she was unexpectedly laid off. With no savings to fall back on, she struggled financially. This experience taught her the importance of an emergency fund. Once she found a new job, Priya prioritized building a six-month expense cushion, ensuring she'd be better prepared for unforeseen financial challenges in the future.

3. **Impulse Purchases**: Carlos was prone to impulse buying. After accumulating a significant amount of debt from numerous unnecessary purchases, he realized the impact of his actions. He then adopted the 48-hour rule, where he'd wait for two days before making any substantial purchase. This pause allowed him to differentiate between wants and needs, dramatically improving his spending habits.

4. **Not Reviewing Financial Statements**: Aisha seldom reviewed her monthly bank and credit card statements. One day, she discovered she'd been paying for a subscription service she no longer used for over a year. Recognizing

her oversight, Aisha started a monthly ritual of reviewing all her financial statements, catching discrepancies, and ensuring she wasn't wasting money.

Here are several quotes that emphasize this sentiment:

1. **Warren Buffett**
   - **Quote**: "I make plenty of mistakes and I'll make plenty more mistakes, too. That's part of the game. You just have to make sure that the right things overcome the wrong."
   - **Implication**: Even the best in the investment world like Buffett make mistakes. The key is to ensure that the successes outshine the failures and to learn from each misstep.

2. **George Soros**
   - **Quote**: "It's not whether you're right or wrong, but how much money you make when you're right and how much you lose when you're wrong."
   - **Implication**: In the financial world, mistakes are inevitable. However, what's crucial is how you manage your wins and losses. Learning from errors and optimizing successes can shape your financial journey.

3. **Robert Kiyosaki** (Author of "Rich Dad Poor Dad")
   - **Quote**: "Winners are not afraid of losing. But losers are. Failure is part of the process of success. People who avoid failure also avoid success."
   - **Implication**: Embracing failures and mistakes as a part of the growth process is essential. Avoiding mistakes entirely may also mean missing out on major growth opportunities.

4. **Thomas Edison**

- ○ **Quote**: "I have not failed. I've just found 10,000 ways that won't work."
- ○ **Implication**: While Edison isn't primarily known for financial wisdom, this mindset is golden for investors. Each mistake is a stepping stone to finding the methods that do work.

5. **Peter Lynch** (Legendary Mutual Fund Manager)
   - ○ **Quote**: "In this business, if you're good, you're right six times out of ten. You're never going to be right nine times out of ten."
   - ○ **Implication**: Perfection is not the goal in financial endeavours. Embracing and learning from the times you're wrong is equally, if not more, valuable.

Financial mistakes, big or small, are inevitable. However, the key lies in how one responds to them. By adopting a mindset that views these mistakes as valuable lessons, individuals can not only avoid repeating them but also use these experiences as a foundation for smarter financial decisions in the future. Embracing failures as part of the learning curve makes the journey to financial freedom more resilient and informed.

PRINCIPLE 66

Negotiate for better deals

Negotiate for better deals and save money in the long run.

The ability to negotiate effectively is a vital skill when it comes to wealth creation and the journey towards financial freedom.

1. **Understanding Value Over Price**:
    - O *Example*: Imagine you're purchasing a house. The asking price is $500,000, but after inspecting it and comparing it with market rates, you believe it's worth $450,000. Negotiating can help you get the property for what it's truly worth, not just the price tag it's been given.
    - O *Long-Term Impact*: Over a lifetime, saving on big-ticket purchases like homes can equate to hundreds of thousands of dollars, if not more.

2. **Incremental Savings Add Up**:
    - O *Example*: Let's say you run a business and frequently deal with suppliers. By negotiating even a 5% decrease in costs with your primary supplier, you might save $10,000 annually.
    - O *Long-Term Impact*: Over 20 years, that's $200,000 saved just by negotiating effectively.

3. **Job Offers and Salaries**:
   - *Example*: When offered a job with a $70,000 salary, you decide to negotiate for $75,000. If accepted, that's an additional $5,000 a year.
   - *Long-Term Impact*: Over a 40-year career, with the magic of compound interest and annual increases, negotiating that initial salary could mean an additional several hundred thousand dollars in earnings.

4. **Flexibility and Terms**:
   - *Example*: You're signing up for a new service (let's say a software subscription). By negotiating, you might not just get a lower price but also more flexible terms, like the ability to cancel anytime or getting additional features at no cost.
   - *Long-Term Impact*: Such flexibility can prove invaluable, allowing you to adapt to changing circumstances without incurring penalties or being stuck with services that no longer suit your needs.

5. **Avoiding Unnecessary Costs**:
   - *Example*: You have a medical bill that seems higher than expected. After reviewing and negotiating, you discover some services were mistakenly added. By discussing, you have them removed and reduce the bill by $500.
   - *Long-Term Impact*: Over time, actively reviewing and negotiating such bills can save a significant amount, allowing those funds to be directed towards investments or other wealth-building avenues.

the principles of negotiation is timeless and spans various disciplines, including finance. Here are some quotations from notable figures that underscore the essence of negotiation, particularly in the context of wealth-building and achieving financial freedom:

1. **Chester L. Karrass:**
   - **Quote:** "In business, you don't get what you deserve, you get what you negotiate."
   - **Implication:** Your worth in business isn't just determined by your value or merit, but by your ability to negotiate effectively. Over a lifetime, stronger negotiations can lead to significantly better financial outcomes.

2. **Warren Buffett:**
   - **Quote:** "Price is what you pay. Value is what you get."
   - **Implication:** Negotiation revolves around discerning the true value of something, rather than just accepting the price presented. This principle encourages us to seek value in our financial decisions and ensure that we aren't overpaying.

3. **Roger Dawson:**
   - **Quote:** "You will never get more than you negotiate. Ask for more, settle for less."
   - **Implication:** Setting a higher starting point in negotiations gives you more room to work with, ultimately leading to better financial outcomes in the long run.

Negotiation isn't just about immediate savings or gains—it's a long-term strategy. Those who cultivate the skill of negotiation and apply it consistently can significantly impact their financial trajectories. Over time, these negotiated savings and gains compound, accelerating the journey to financial freedom. Whether it's saving on daily purchases, securing a higher salary, or obtaining more favourable terms on contracts, the art of negotiation is an indispensable tool in the wealth-building toolkit.

Negotiate: never split the difference

The phrase "Never split the difference" is popularly associated with the former FBI hostage negotiator Chris Voss and his book of the same name. The essence of this principle is a shift away from the classic negotiation advice, which often suggests finding a middle ground or a compromise. Instead, Voss emphasizes a more nuanced approach to negotiation. Let's delve into the meaning:

1. **Understanding Emotion and Logic**:
    - *Example*: In buying a home, instead of immediately discussing prices, you might want to understand the seller's motivation. Are they looking for a quick sale due to a job relocation? If so, you might have room to negotiate more aggressively.
    - *Impact*: By understanding their emotional motivations and not just focusing on splitting the price difference, you could secure a better deal.
2. **"No" Can Be More Powerful Than "Yes"**:
    - *Example*: If a vendor pitches a service to you for $10,000 and you feel it's worth $8,000, instead of immediately countering, you could express doubt or reluctance. This might lead the vendor to drop the price without you even offering your number.

- ○ *Impact*: By allowing the other party to feel they have control and letting them come to conclusions on their own, you can often get a more favourable outcome.

3. **Calibrated Questions**:
   - ○ *Example*: When renegotiating a lease contract, instead of making a statement like "We need a 10% reduction in rent," you could ask, "How can we work together to adjust the rent considering the current market conditions?"
   - ○ *Impact*: Such questions make the other party think and often lead to solutions that are more favourable to you. It's not about splitting the difference but about collaboratively finding a solution that tilers towards your desired outcome.

4. **Acknowledge Their Fears**:
   - ○ *Example*: In a salary negotiation, if an employer can't meet your desired salary, instead of pushing the number, try understanding their reservations. Maybe they're afraid of setting a precedent or straining their budget. By acknowledging this and offering solutions, like a performance bonus, you might get a package that meets your compensation goals in a different way.
   - ○ *Impact*: By addressing and alleviating their concerns, you can often find alternative ways to reach your desired outcome without "splitting the difference."

5. **Silence is Golden**:
   - ○ *Example*: If you're selling a product and the buyer says the price is too high, instead of immediately lowering it, remain silent for a moment. This can make the other party uncomfortable, leading them to fill the silence, possibly by justifying why they might pay the

higher price or revealing what they're actually willing to pay.

- ○ *Impact*: Silence can be a powerful tool in negotiations, leading the other party to reveal more than they intended, giving you an advantage.

"Never split the difference" is about taking a more strategic and psychological approach to negotiations rather than just aiming for a quick compromise. It's about recognizing that each negotiation is unique, with hidden dynamics and variables, and that by deeply engaging with and understanding the counterpart, you can find solutions that might not be immediately obvious. In many cases, this results in better outcomes than simply splitting differences.

PRINCIPLE 68

Avoid peer pressure spending

Spend according to your financial goals, not others' standards.

The principle of "Avoiding peer pressure spending" emphasizes the importance of making financial decisions based on your own goals and priorities, rather than succumbing to societal norms, trends, or the expectations of others. Let's delve deeper into this principle and understand its significance in wealth creation and achieving financial freedom.

1. **Influence of Peer Pressure:**
   - In the era of social media, it's easy to see what others are doing, buying, or experiencing. This constant bombardment can lead to a phenomenon called "lifestyle inflation" where people increase their expenses as their discretionary income rises, especially when they see their peers living a more luxurious life.
   - For instance, seeing friends on exotic vacations or driving high-end cars might push someone to take on unnecessary debt or spend beyond their means to "keep up."

2. **Financial Individuality:**
   - Everyone's financial situation, goals, and values are unique. What makes sense for one person may not be right for another. For example, while some prioritize

homeownership, others might find value in traveling or investing in experiences.

○ John might buy a brand-new luxury car because it's a status symbol in his circle, while Emily opts for a modest used car, choosing to invest the difference in stocks.

3.   **The Impact of Succumbing to Peer Pressure**:

○ Giving in to peer pressure can delay or derail your financial goals. If you're constantly updating your wardrobe to match the latest trends your friends are into, or frequently dining at upscale places because that's where your peers hang out, you're diverting funds that could be used to pay down debt, invest, or save.

○ Example: If Jake spends an extra $300 a month on branded clothing to fit in, over a year, that's $3,600. Over a decade, without considering potential interest, that's $36,000!

4.   **Benefits of Resisting Peer Pressure**:

○ By focusing on your financial goals and not on what others are doing, you can allocate your resources more efficiently. This means faster debt repayment, more significant savings, and investments that can grow over time due to compounding interest.

○ Sarah, for instance, might resist the urge to upgrade her phone every year like her colleagues do. By doing so, she can invest the money she saves, leading to potentially higher returns in the long run.

5.   **The Psychological Aspect**:

○ Avoiding peer pressure spending isn't just about money; it's about mental well-being. Constant comparison with others can lead to feelings of inadequacy, stress, or even depression. Making financial decisions based on personal goals rather than societal standards promotes a sense of achievement, satisfaction, and peace of mind.

Here are some financial principles derived from famous quotes that align with this mindset:

1. **Live Below Your Means:**
   - ○ "Too many people spend money they haven't earned, to buy things they don't want, to impress people they don't like." — *Will Rogers*
   - ○ Interpretation: Don't let external pressures force you into a lifestyle you can't afford. Understand the difference between needs and wants.

2. **Know Your Worth:**
   - ○ "Rich people believe 'I create my life'. Poor people believe 'Life happens to me'." — *T. Harv Eker*
   - ○ Interpretation: Take control of your financial destiny. Don't let societal pressures dictate your spending habits.

3. **The Illusion of Materialism:**
   - ○ "Too many people spend money they earned... to buy things they don't want... to impress people that they don't like." — *Will Rogers*
   - ○ Interpretation: Trying to keep up with others or give off a certain image can lead to wasteful spending. Prioritize your financial health and long-term goals.

4. **Prioritize Financial Education:**
   - ○ "An investment in knowledge pays the best interest." — *Benjamin Franklin*

- ○ Interpretation: Instead of succumbing to societal pressures, invest time in understanding finances and money management to make informed decisions.

5. **Value Experiences Over Things**:
   - ○ "It's not how much money you make, but how much money you keep, how hard it works for you, and how many generations you keep it for." — *Robert Kiyosaki*
   - ○ Interpretation: Avoid spending on fleeting trends. Instead, focus on building and maintaining wealth over time, according to your standards and goals.

Avoiding peer pressure spending is about understanding that your financial journey is personal. It's a marathon, not a sprint, and the only person you should be in competition with is your past self. By making deliberate and informed choices, aligned with your financial objectives, you lay a solid foundation for wealth creation and financial freedom.

Be patient

Successful wealth-building takes time and discipline.

The principle of patience is essential in the journey of wealth creation and financial freedom. It underscores the significance of a long-term perspective, consistency, and resilience in financial strategies. Let's delve deeper into this principle.

ELABORATION:

1. **Understanding the Power of Compounding**:
   - **Example**: Imagine two individuals, Amy and Bob. Amy starts investing $300 every month from the age of 25 till 35 and then stops contributing but leaves her money to grow. Bob, on the other hand, begins investing the same amount monthly from age 35 until retirement at 65. By retirement, even though Amy invested for only 10 years and Bob for 30, due to the power of compounding, Amy might have a larger fund than Bob if the rate of return is consistent. This scenario highlights the advantage of starting early and patiently letting investments grow.

2. **Avoiding Emotional Financial Decisions**:
   - The stock market is inherently volatile. Investors who react impulsively to short-term market fluctuations

often sell low and buy high, which is detrimental to building wealth.

- ○ **Example**: During a market downturn, an impatient investor might panic and sell their stocks, incurring losses. A patient investor, understanding market cycles, might hold onto their investments, or even buy more at lower prices, thus benefiting when the market eventually recovers.

3. **Benefits of Delayed Gratification**:
   - ○ Patience often means resisting the urge for immediate rewards in favor of future benefits.
   - ○ **Example**: Consider Jack, who gets a bonus of $5,000. He could use that money to buy a luxury watch immediately, or he could invest it. If he opts for the latter and earns an average annual return of 7%, in 30 years, that $5,000 could grow to over $38,000 without any additional contributions.

4. **Diversified Investments and the Long Game**:
   - ○ A diversified portfolio spread across different asset classes can be a buffer against market volatility. While some assets might underperform in the short term, they might be top performers in the long run.
   - ○ **Example**: If Sarah invests in a mix of stocks, bonds, and real estate, even if the stock market has a downturn, her investments in real estate and bonds might still offer stability. Over time, with patience, her overall portfolio can see balanced growth.

5. **Building Habits and Discipline**:
   - ○ Consistent savings and investment, even in small amounts, can lead to significant wealth over time. It's the discipline of routinely setting aside money that, over decades, can lead to substantial growth.

- ○ **Example**: If Michael sets aside just $200 every month from age 25 at a 6% annual return, by age 65, he could have over $500,000 from contributions totalling just $96,000.

6. **Resilience in the Face of Setbacks**:
   - ○ Every financial journey has its challenges, whether it's a loss of employment, market downturns, or unexpected expenses. Patience is crucial in navigating these challenges without derailing long-term financial goals.
   - ○ **Example**: After a job loss, Lisa might dip into her savings to cover immediate expenses. But instead of draining all her investments, she remains patient, cuts non-essential expenses, and actively seeks new employment, ensuring her long-term financial plans remain largely on track.

Patience in wealth-building is not about inaction but about informed, deliberate actions coupled with the wisdom to understand that significant growth and financial freedom are often the fruits of time and unwavering discipline.

Reinvest windfalls

Reinvest windfalls: Put unexpected cash windfalls into investments or debt repayment.

A windfall is a sudden and often unexpected financial gain. It could arise from various sources like a lottery win, an inheritance, a tax refund, a bonus at work, or even finding a valuable item. While the immediate reaction for many is to spend this newfound wealth on luxuries or long-desired items, reinvesting it can have long-lasting benefits and significantly contribute to achieving financial freedom.

WHY REINVEST OR REPAY DEBT?

1. **Compound Growth**: Money invested wisely can grow exponentially over time, thanks to the power of compound interest. Even if the windfall isn't substantial, it can accumulate into a sizable amount given enough time.

2. **Reduce Financial Stress**: Paying off debts, especially high-interest ones, can relieve financial stress. You end up saving on future interest payments, effectively making your windfall grow in value.

3. **Safety Net**: By reinvesting a windfall, you can bolster your emergency fund, ensuring that sudden expenses or disruptions in income don't derail your financial goals.

4. **Leverage Opportunities**: Having extra capital from a windfall can be used to take advantage of investment opportunities that might have previously been out of reach.

EXAMPLES:

1. **Inheritance**: Jane received an inheritance of $50,000. Instead of buying a new car, she decided to invest it in a diversified stock portfolio. Over 20 years, with an average return of 7%, this sum could grow to over $193,000 without adding any more money.

2. **Bonus**: Mark got a year-end bonus of $5,000. He chose to use $3,000 to pay off his high-interest credit card debt, saving hundreds in interest payments over the next couple of years. He then took the remaining $2,000 and added it to his retirement account.

3. **Tax Refund**: Emily received a $2,500 tax refund. She immediately put it into her emergency fund, ensuring she wouldn't have to rely on credit if unexpected expenses arose.

4. **Lottery Win**: Raj won $10,000 in a local lottery. Instead of going on a lavish vacation, he used half to pay off his student loan and invested the other half in real estate, which provided him a steady rental income.

While it's tempting to spend windfalls immediately, treating them as a foundation for future financial stability can lead to sustainable wealth and financial freedom. It's not about denying oneself pleasures, but about optimizing long-term gains and stability over short-term gratifications. The decision between spending, saving, investing, or debt repayment will vary depending on individual circumstances, but the principle of being strategic with windfalls remains consistent.

Use technology

Utilize apps and tools to track expenses and investments.

This principle emphasizes the pivotal role of modern technology in streamlining financial management and investment strategies. As we move into an increasingly digital age, leveraging these tools can make a significant difference in wealth accumulation and financial planning.

ELABORATION ON THE STATEMENT:

1. **Simplified Budgeting**: Before the age of technology, budgeting involved tedious processes of maintaining physical ledgers or manually entering expenses into spreadsheets. Now, with budgeting apps, users can link their bank accounts, set spending categories, and monitor their financial habits in real-time.

    ○ **Example**: Apps like Mint or YNAB (You Need A Budget) automatically categorize and track spending, set monthly budgets, and send alerts when one is nearing or exceeding their budget limits. This proactive approach helps inculcate disciplined spending habits.

2. **Real-time Investment Tracking**: Rather than waiting for quarterly reports or checking various platforms

individually, investment apps consolidate portfolio data, providing real-time insights and performance metrics.

- ○ **Example**: Platforms like Robinhood or E*TRADE not only allow for stock trading but also offer analytical tools, real-time market data, and insights to keep investors informed.

3. **Robo-Advisors for Tailored Investment Strategies**: Robo-advisors use algorithms to determine the best investment strategy based on an individual's risk tolerance and financial goals. This automation ensures objective, data-driven decision-making, reducing emotional or impulsive investment decisions.

- ○ **Example**: Betterment and Wealth front are robot-advisory platforms that construct personalized portfolios, rebalance them when necessary, and even optimize for tax efficiency.

4. **Expense and Debt Management**: Some apps are specifically designed to highlight areas of excessive spending or to help pay down debts more efficiently.

- ○ **Example**: Apps like Tally or Qoins analyse users' financial profiles and optimize the best strategies to pay down credit card debts or round up purchases to the nearest dollar, putting the spare change towards debt.

5. **Digital Financial Education**: Various platforms offer educational resources, tutorials, and news updates to keep users informed about market trends, investment strategies, or personal finance best practices.

- ○ **Example**: Investopedia Academy or Khan Academy's finance courses are platforms where individuals can learn about stocks, bonds, financial planning, and more.

6. **Automated Savings**: Some apps automatically divert a part of a user's income or round up change from purchases into savings or investment accounts.

    ○   **Example**: Acorns is an app that rounds up the user's purchases and invests the change in a diversified portfolio, making the process of investing spare change seamless.

7. **Safety and Security**: Modern financial apps employ advanced encryption methods, ensuring that users' data and money are secure. This level of security might be harder to achieve with traditional, physical means of money management.

By harnessing the power of technology, individuals are better equipped to manage their finances, make informed decisions, and set themselves on a path to financial freedom. From day-to-day budgeting to long-term investment strategies, technology offers tools and resources that were previously unimaginable. In the pursuit of wealth creation and financial freedom, it's not just about how much one earns but also how effectively one manages and grows their wealth— and technology plays a central role in that journey.

Protect your financial data

Keep sensitive information secure to avoid fraud.

The importance of safeguarding financial data in our increasingly digital age cannot be overstated. Let's dive deeper into the statement:

Protect your financial data: Keep sensitive information secure to avoid fraud.

ELABORATION:

Protecting financial data doesn't only mean guarding one's money. It also involves preserving one's reputation, creditworthiness, and avoiding the time-consuming, often stressful process of recuperating from identity theft or financial fraud.

In an era where digital transactions are prevalent, there are numerous entry points for hackers or fraudsters to gain unauthorized access to personal financial information. Such access can lead to unauthorized transactions, ruined credit, or even more complex forms of identity theft.

EXAMPLES:

1. **Online Shopping:**
    ○ *Scenario:* John regularly shops online. One day, he receives an email claiming to be from one of his

favourite online stores, asking him to update his payment details. Without thinking, he clicks on the link and updates his information.

○ *Result:* Over the next month, he notices unauthorized transactions from his bank account. John fell victim to a phishing email.

○ *Protection Measure:* John could have protected his data by verifying the email's authenticity, checking the sender's email address, and reaching out to the company directly rather than clicking on the link.

2. **Using Public Wi-Fi:**

○ *Scenario:* Emily, while waiting at the airport, decides to check her investment portfolio. She connects to the airport's public Wi-Fi and logs into her investment account.

○ *Result:* Hackers on unsecured public networks can use various tools to intercept data. Emily's login details might get captured, leading to unauthorized access.

○ *Protection Measure:* Emily should use a virtual private network (VPN) while accessing sensitive information on public networks. VPNs encrypt data, making it harder for hackers to intercept.

3. **Lost Wallet:**

○ *Scenario:* David loses his wallet containing his credit cards, driver's license, and other important information.

○ *Result:* Besides the immediate financial loss, David is at risk of identity theft if someone uses his driver's license and credit card information to impersonate him.

○ *Protection Measure:* Immediately upon realizing his wallet is missing, David should notify his bank and credit card companies to freeze or cancel his cards. He should also monitor his credit reports for unusual activity.

4. **Using Weak or Common Passwords:**
   ○ *Scenario:* Maria uses her birthdate as the password for her online banking.
   ○ *Result:* A hacker trying to gain access to her account may attempt using common passwords or details available from her public profiles, like her birthdate.
   ○ *Protection Measure:* Maria should use strong, unique passwords for her financial accounts. Password managers can help generate and store complex passwords.

Here are some famous quotes and principles that resonate with the concept of safeguarding financial data:

1. **"Trust, but verify."** - *Ronald Reagan*
   ○ Principle: Even when dealing with trusted institutions or individuals, always double-check and ensure that your financial data remains protected.

2. **"An ounce of prevention is worth a pound of cure."** - *Benjamin Franklin*
   ○ Principle: Investing time and resources now to safeguard your financial data can save much more time, money, and stress in the event of potential future breaches or fraud.

3. **"Caution is the eldest child of wisdom."** - *Victor Hugo*
   ○ Principle: Wisdom directs us to be careful, especially when it comes to crucial aspects like our financial data.

4. **"Privacy – like eating and breathing – is one of life's basic requirements."** - *Katherine Neville*

○ Principle: Just as essential needs must be protected and preserved, so should our financial privacy.

5. **"In this treacherous world, nothing is the truth nor a lie. Everything depends on the colour of the crystal through which one sees it."** - *Pedro Calderón de la Barca*

○ Principle: Always approach financial dealings with a lens of scepticism. Protecting your financial data means being alert to potential misrepresentations or fraud.

In essence, protecting financial data requires constant vigilance and an understanding of the potential threats in today's digital age. With the right practices, tools, and awareness, one can significantly reduce the risk of financial fraud, ensuring a smoother path to achieving financial freedom.

Know your net worth

Calculate your net worth regularly to track your financial progress.

Net worth is a snapshot of your financial health. In its simplest form, it's calculated by subtracting your total liabilities (what you owe) from your total assets (what you own). This single figure provides a clear picture of your current financial position and is a key indicator of your financial progress over time.

WHY IS KNOWING YOUR NET WORTH IMPORTANT?

1. **Foundation for Financial Planning**: Just as a doctor needs to understand your vital statistics before giving health advice, understanding your net worth is crucial for making informed financial decisions.

2. **Measure of Financial Health**: Your net worth can serve as a barometer for your overall financial health. If it's growing over time, you're likely making good financial choices. If it's shrinking, you might be living above your means or not investing wisely.

3. **Goal Setting**: Knowing your net worth can help you set tangible financial goals. For instance, if you want to have a net worth of $500,000 by age 40, tracking your net worth can help you see if you're on course to achieve that goal.

EXAMPLES OF ITS APPLICATION:

1. **Real Estate Decisions**: Let's say Jane owns a house worth $300,000, but she still owes $200,000 on her mortgage. Her equity in the house (an asset) is $100,000. By calculating her net worth, Jane realizes that a significant portion of her assets is tied up in her home. She may decide to sell and downsize to free up some capital, or she might choose to accelerate her mortgage payments to increase her home equity.

2. **Investment Evaluation**: Tom has a stock portfolio worth $50,000 and no debt. Over the years, by tracking his net worth and the contribution of his portfolio to it, Tom can gauge the performance of his investments. If his net worth isn't growing as he anticipates, he might reconsider his investment strategy.

3. **Retirement Planning**: Sarah calculates her net worth in order to judge whether she has enough assets to maintain her lifestyle post-retirement. If she sees her net worth is less than desired, she might decide to work a few more years or look into other income sources.

4. **Debt Management**: Raj has student loans, a car loan, and credit card debt, which collectively amount to $80,000. His assets, including savings, some stocks, and a car, amount to $60,000. With a negative net worth of -$20,000, this can be a wake-up call for Raj. He may opt for a debt consolidation strategy, look for additional income sources, or cut unnecessary expenses.

Here are some financial principles inspired by famous quotes that relate to the importance of knowing one's net worth:

1. **"What gets measured gets managed."** - Peter Drucker
   - ○ Interpretation: Regularly measuring and tracking your net worth will ensure you're always aware of your financial standing, allowing you to manage and improve it effectively.

2. **"Don't tell me where your priorities are. Show me where you spend your money, and I'll tell you what they are."** - James W. Frick
   - ○ Interpretation: Knowing your net worth is a tangible way to understand where your money is allocated and can provide insight into your true financial priorities.

3. **"Your net worth to the world is usually determined by what remains after your bad habits are subtracted from your good ones."** - Benjamin Franklin
   - ○ Interpretation: Your financial habits, both good and bad, ultimately shape your net worth. Knowing where you stand can motivate improvements in financial behaviour.

4. **"It's not how much money you make, but how much money you keep, how hard it works for you, and how many generations you keep it for."** - Robert Kiyosaki
   - ○ Interpretation: Earnings are only one component of net worth. How you manage, invest, and preserve wealth is essential for long-term financial success.

5. **"The richest man is not he who has the most, but he who needs the least."** - Unknown
   - ○ Interpretation: Understanding net worth is not just about accumulating assets but also about managing and reducing liabilities, leading to financial independence.

Knowing and tracking your net worth is a bit like having a GPS for your financial journey. It tells you where you are now, helps direct where you need to go, and shows you how far you've come. Regularly assessing this figure ensures you stay on the right financial path, make necessary adjustments along the way, and ultimately achieve your wealth and financial freedom goals.

PRINCIPLE 74

Save for big purchases

Plan and save for significant expenses instead of borrowing.

The principle of saving for big purchases revolves around the idea of disciplined financial planning, patience, and foresight. Rather than immediately satisfying a want or need through borrowing, one sets aside money over time to make that purchase outright. This approach not only minimizes or eliminates interest payments (which can considerably add to the cost of the purchase when borrowing), but it also encourages thoughtful spending and reduces the risks associated with debt.

EXAMPLES:

1. **Buying a Car:**
    - ○ *Borrowing:* John sees a car he likes priced at $20,000. He doesn't have the money upfront, so he takes a car loan. Over a 5-year loan term with an interest rate of 5%, he ends up paying around $22,645 (including $2,645 as interest). Plus, he's bound by monthly obligations regardless of how his financial situation might change.
    - ○ *Saving:* On the other hand, Sarah wants a similar car. Instead of taking out a loan, she decides to save $333 a month for 5 years. By the end of that period, she has the $20,000 she needs, purchases her car outright,

and pays no interest. Moreover, during those 5 years, she's free from any financial obligation and can adjust her savings rate as needed.

2. **Vacations:**
   - ○ *Borrowing:* Alex decides to take a trip to Europe and puts everything - flight, hotel, activities - on his credit card, totalling $5,000. It takes him two years to pay it off with a 15% interest rate, costing him an extra $750 in interest.
   - ○ *Saving:* Maria dreams of that European trip too. She plans her journey two years in advance, setting aside $208 every month. In two years, she has saved up $5,000, books her vacation, and has no debts when she returns.

3. **Home Renovations:**
   - ○ *Borrowing:* Lisa wants to renovate her kitchen and takes out a personal loan of $10,000 with an interest rate of 7% over 3 years. She ends up paying $1,100 in interest alone.
   - ○ *Saving:* Mark, who has a similar kitchen renovation in mind, decides to wait for a year, saving $917 a month. After a year, he has the $11,000 he needs for his kitchen, without any debt or interest payments.

BENEFITS:

1. **No Debt Stress:** When you save for a significant purchase, you avoid the constant stress and strain that come with monthly loan payments.
2. **Flexibility:** If a financial emergency arises, you're not bound by the obligations of a loan repayment.
3. **True Cost:** When you save, you pay the actual cost of an item, not an inflated price that includes interest.

4. **Discipline and Financial Growth:** The discipline needed to save consistently can spill over into other areas of your finances, leading to better overall money management.

Planning and saving for big purchases instead of borrowing is a foundational principle for building wealth and achieving financial freedom. By adopting this principle, one can avoid unnecessary debts, cultivate financial discipline, and realize genuine, long-lasting satisfaction from their purchases.

Pursuit of Continuous Financial Education and Investment Knowledge

Continuously educate yourself about personal finance and investing.

Financial literacy is the ability to understand how money works, including how one earns it, manages it, invests it, and donates it to help others. It is a cornerstone of building wealth and achieving financial freedom. Without a strong understanding of finances, people often find themselves in cyclical patterns of debt, poor investments, and missed opportunities.

EXAMPLES:

1. **Budgeting:**
   - ○ *Lack of Knowledge:* James never learned the importance of budgeting. He earns a decent salary but often finds himself living paycheck to paycheck, wondering where his money goes every month.
   - ○ *With Financial Literacy:* Samantha took a short course on personal finance and learned about budgeting. She tracks her expenses, categorizes them, and sets limits on discretionary spending. This allows her to save a substantial portion of her income every month.

2. **Investing:**

    ○ *Lack of Knowledge:* Emily hears about a hot stock tip from a friend and decides to invest a large chunk of her savings without doing any research. The stock tanks, and she loses a significant amount of money.

    ○ *With Financial Literacy:* David, before investing, reads about the company, checks its financial health, leadership, market position, and future prospects. He diversifies his investments to spread and reduce risks. Over time, his careful and educated approach yields a positive return on investment.

3. **Understanding Debt:**

    ○ *Lack of Knowledge:* Carlos racks up credit card debt due to unchecked spending. He pays just the minimum amount due each month, not realizing the high interest accumulating on his outstanding balance.

    ○ *With Financial Literacy:* Nina understands the implications of high-interest credit card debt. She uses her credit card judiciously, always paying the full balance each month, thereby avoiding unnecessary interest charges.

FAMOUS QUOTES RELATING TO FINANCIAL LITERACY:

1. **"An investment in knowledge pays the best interest."** - Benjamin Franklin

    ○ Principle: Education, especially in finance, gives the best returns.

2. **"It's not how much money you make, but how much money you keep, how hard it works for you, and how many generations you keep it for."** - Robert Kiyosaki

    ○ Principle: Financial literacy is crucial not just for earning but for retaining and growing wealth.

3. **"The stock market is filled with individuals who know the price of everything, but the value of nothing."** - Philip Fisher
   - ○ Principle: True understanding of finance goes beyond surface-level numbers.

4. **"The number one problem in today's generation and the economy is the lack of financial literacy."** - Alan Greenspan
   - ○ Principle: Understanding finances is essential for both personal wealth and the broader economy.

5. **"Opportunities come infrequently. When it rains gold, put out the bucket, not the thimble."** - Warren Buffett
   - ○ Principle: Being financially literate allows you to recognize and seize opportunities when they arise.

In essence, being financially literate equips an individual with the tools and knowledge to make informed decisions, maximize earning potential, and navigate the complexities of the financial world. Continuous education in personal finance and investing is a valuable investment in itself, offering compounding benefits over time.

Separate needs from wants

Prioritize essential expenses over discretionary spending.

Drawing a clear line between needs and wants is a foundational principle in personal finance. While "needs" are the basics we can't live without (like food, shelter, and basic healthcare), "wants" are things that enhance our lives but aren't absolutely necessary (like the latest tech gadget or luxury vacations). Distinguishing between the two and prioritizing essential expenses can significantly impact one's financial health, allowing for better money management, increased savings, and eventually, financial freedom.

EXAMPLES:

1. **Housing:**
   - *Need:* Rita is moving to a new city for work and needs a place to stay. She identifies a comfortable, safe apartment within her budget close to her workplace.
   - *Want:* Rita also spots a luxurious penthouse with a scenic view in a high-end neighbourhood. It's tempting but way beyond her budget. If she chooses this, she might struggle with monthly expenses or be unable to save.

2. **Transportation:**
   - ○ *Need:* Jake needs a vehicle for his daily commute, so he buys a reliable, fuel-efficient car that suits his requirements and budget.
   - ○ *Want:* Jake has always dreamt of owning a high-end sports car. While it's tempting, it's also expensive and not practical for daily commuting. If he buys it, he'll also have higher insurance rates and fuel costs.

3. **Clothing:**
   - ○ *Need:* Sarah needs winter clothing as she's relocating to a colder region. She buys quality winter essentials that will last for years.
   - ○ *Want:* While shopping, Sarah spots a designer dress that's trendy but very expensive and not suitable for cold weather. Buying it would mean cutting back on other essential purchases.

4. **Dining:**
   - ○ *Need:* Alex is hungry and needs lunch. He opts for a balanced meal that's filling and reasonably priced.
   - ○ *Want:* Alex also sees a gourmet restaurant nearby. Dining there regularly might mean delicious food, but it could dent his monthly budget significantly.

5. **Entertainment:**
   - ○ *Need:* Maria enjoys watching movies to relax. She subscribes to an online streaming service, giving her access to a wide range of films for a modest monthly fee.
   - ○ *Want:* Maria also considers buying a state-of-the-art home theatre system. While it promises an immersive experience, it's not essential and comes with a hefty price tag.

Being able to differentiate between needs and wants doesn't mean one should never indulge in their wants. It's about being mindful of financial limitations and ensuring that essential expenses are covered first. Over time, as one's financial situation improves, there will be more room to enjoy discretionary spending without compromising financial stability or goals. After all, financial freedom is not about deprivation; it's about making informed decisions that align with both current needs and future aspirations.

Invest in what you understand

Avoid complex investments without proper knowledge.

One of the cardinal rules of investing is to put your money in businesses or assets that you understand thoroughly. Complex investments might seem enticing due to potential high returns, but they can also carry high risks, especially if the investor doesn't have a solid grasp of the underlying mechanisms. By sticking to what you understand, you minimize the risks associated with unforeseen challenges or market changes, ensuring more informed and strategic decisions.

EXAMPLES:

1. **Tech Stocks:**
   - *Understanding:* Liam, a software engineer, has firsthand knowledge of cloud technologies. He understands their potential, growth, and the competitive landscape. Therefore, investing in stocks of cloud technology companies makes sense for him.
   - *No Understanding:* However, if Liam comes across a biotech stock that promises revolutionary breakthroughs, but he has zero understanding of the science behind it or the competitive landscape, it might be a riskier venture for him.
2. **Real Estate:**

○ *Understanding:* Priya has been a real estate agent for a decade. She knows her local property market, the factors influencing property prices, and can spot undervalued properties. It would be logical for her to invest in real estate in her region.

○ *No Understanding:* If Priya suddenly decides to invest in foreign real estate markets, where property laws, market conditions, and buyer behaviors are unfamiliar to her, she may encounter unexpected challenges and risks.

3. **Cryptocurrency:**

○ *Understanding:* Alex has been studying cryptocurrencies, understands blockchain technology, and is aware of the factors affecting crypto prices. Investing a portion of his funds in crypto might be a calculated risk for him.

○ *No Understanding:* On the contrary, if Alex's friend Mark, who barely understands digital wallets, decides to jump into the crypto market just because it's the latest trend, he's stepping into a potentially volatile environment blindfolded.

4. **Commodity Trading:**

○ *Understanding:* Clara has worked in the oil and gas industry and knows the factors affecting oil prices. Investing in oil futures might be a suitable avenue for her.

○ *No Understanding:* If Clara suddenly starts investing in agricultural commodities like soybean futures without understanding the factors affecting soybean prices (like weather patterns, global demand, etc.), she's in murkier waters.

Warren Buffett, one of the most successful investors of all time, once said, "Never invest in a business you cannot understand." This advice is a testament to the importance of knowledge and understanding in investment decisions. While every investment carries a degree of risk, understanding the asset or business reduces the unpredictability and allows for a more strategic, informed approach. It ensures that you're not just throwing money into the dark but are placing it where you can see a clear path to potential growth and returns.

Protect against inflation

Invest in assets that preserve purchasing power.

Inflation refers to the gradual increase in prices over time, which consequently erodes the purchasing power of money. If your money isn't growing at a rate that's at least equal to inflation, you're effectively losing wealth. Investing in assets that have historically outpaced inflation can help preserve (and even grow) your purchasing power, ensuring that the money you've saved today will still have a significant value in the future.

EXAMPLES:

1. **Real Estate:**
   O *Preserving Purchasing Power:* Over the long term, property prices have generally risen at rates that exceed inflation. Let's say Emily buys a house for $250,000. In 20 years, due to inflation, everyday goods and services might cost twice as much. But if the house's value has tripled in that time frame, Emily has not only kept up with inflation but has also increased her purchasing power.

2. **Stocks:**
   O *Preserving Purchasing Power:* Historically, the stock market has provided returns that beat inflation. For instance, if Jake invests $10,000 in a diversified stock

portfolio, and it grows at an average of 7% per year, after accounting for a 3% annual inflation rate, he's still making a real return of 4% annually. Over time, this can significantly outpace the eroding effects of inflation.

3. **Gold and Precious Metals:**
   ○ *Preserving Purchasing Power:* Many investors view gold as a hedge against inflation. For instance, 50 years ago, an ounce of gold could buy a high-quality suit. Today, an ounce of gold can still buy a high-quality suit, despite the price in paper currency being much higher. In this way, gold has preserved its purchasing power.

4. **Treasury Inflation-Protected Securities (TIPS):**
   ○ *Preserving Purchasing Power:* TIPS are government securities that increase in value with inflation and pay interest based on the adjusted principal. So, if Mary invests in TIPS and inflation rises, her investment's principal will rise too, ensuring her returns keep pace with the increasing cost of living.

5. **Rental Property:**
   ○ *Preserving Purchasing Power:* Investing in rental properties can provide cash flow that increases with inflation. If Robert owns a rental property and the cost-of-living rises, he can charge higher rent over the years, ensuring his income from the property keeps up with or exceeds inflation.

Inflation, often termed as the "silent thief," slowly eats away at the value of money. By strategically investing in assets that are resistant to inflation's eroding effects, individuals can ensure that their wealth doesn't just remain static but grows in real terms. This proactive approach towards inflation is crucial for anyone aiming for financial freedom, as it ensures that the wealth, they accumulate today retains its value and purchasing power in the future.

Assess your risk tolerance

Understand how much risk you can comfortably handle.

Risk tolerance is an individual's ability or willingness to endure losses in investment values while pursuing potential rewards. Everyone has different levels of comfort when it comes to taking on risk, and understanding your personal risk tolerance is essential in determining the type of investments that are right for you. Investments that carry higher levels of risk are typically associated with the potential for higher rewards and vice versa.

EXAMPLES:

1. **Conservative Investor - Low Risk Tolerance:**
   - *Scenario:* Jane, a retiree, has saved up enough for her golden years. She wants her money to grow but can't afford significant drops in her investments, as she relies on them for living expenses.
   - *Investment Strategy:* Jane may opt for more stable investments like bonds, money market funds, or CDs. While the returns may be modest, the principal is much safer from the volatility of the stock market.

2. **Aggressive Investor - High Risk Tolerance:**
   - *Scenario:* Alex, in his early 30s, has a stable job and an emergency fund. He's willing to take on more risk for

the potential of higher returns, knowing he has time to recover from any short-term losses.

- ○ *Investment Strategy:* Alex might invest in growth stocks, emerging markets, or even speculative ventures. He accepts the fact that while he could see substantial gains, there's also the potential for significant losses.

3. **Moderate Investor - Moderate Risk Tolerance:**
   - ○ *Scenario:* Kelly, in her mid-40s, has a decent retirement nest and wants a balanced approach. She wants her investments to grow but with some level of stability.
   - ○ *Investment Strategy:* Kelly might have a diversified portfolio containing a mix of stocks and bonds, balancing potential returns with some level of security.

4. **Business Ventures:**
   - ○ *Scenario:* David has an opportunity to invest in a startup. He's enthusiastic but knows that many startups fail.
   - ○ *Decision Making:* Based on his risk tolerance, David might decide to invest a small amount that he's comfortable potentially losing. Alternatively, if he's risk-averse, he might pass on the opportunity altogether.

5. **Property Investment:**
   - ○ *Scenario:* Sarah is considering buying an investment property in an up-and-coming area. The neighbourhood is still in the early stages of gentrification, so there's potential for significant appreciation, but also the risk that the area might not develop as expected.

○ *Decision Making:* If Sarah has a high-risk tolerance, she might go ahead with the purchase, seeing it as a long-term play with substantial upside. However, if she's more conservative, she might choose a property in a more established area with steady, predictable returns.

Understanding one's risk tolerance isn't just about gauging potential returns. It's also about ensuring that your investment decisions align with your financial goals and personal comfort levels. An inappropriate risk level can lead to emotional stress and potentially rash decisions in volatile markets. By properly assessing risk tolerance, individuals can craft investment strategies that not only have the potential to grow wealth but also allow them to sleep soundly at night.

PRINCIPLE 80

Plan for contingencies

Have backup plans for unexpected events.

Contingency planning in personal finance refers to the process of preparing for unexpected events that might negatively affect your financial well-being. Life is unpredictable, and many external factors, such as medical emergencies, job loss, or natural disasters, can derail one's financial progress. By setting up backup plans, you ensure that your journey to financial freedom remains on track, even when faced with adverse events.

EXAMPLES:

1. **Emergency Funds:**
   - *Scenario:* Peter has a steady job and earns a decent income. He manages to save and invest regularly. However, understanding the uncertainties of life, he sets aside three to six months' worth of expenses in an easily accessible savings account.
   - *Outcome:* When the company he works for undergoes restructuring and lays off several employees, including Peter, he isn't immediately worried about his bills. His emergency fund acts as a financial cushion, giving him ample time to find another job without compromising his lifestyle.

2. **Insurance Coverage:**

- ○ *Scenario:* Sarah, a mother of two, understands the importance of protecting her family from unforeseen events. She takes out both life and health insurance policies.
- ○ *Outcome:* Unfortunately, she gets diagnosed with a critical illness. Thanks to her health insurance, the bulk of her medical expenses are covered. Moreover, the life insurance ensures that her family will be financially secure should anything happen to her.

3. **Diversified Investment:**
   - ○ *Scenario:* Alex has $100,000 to invest. Instead of putting all his money into a single stock or business venture, he diversifies across different asset classes, industries, and even geographic regions.
   - ○ *Outcome:* An economic downturn affects one of the sectors he invested in severely. However, since Alex had diversified his investments, only a portion of his portfolio is impacted, thus reducing his overall losses.

4. **Backup Career Skills:**
   - ○ *Scenario:* Maria, a journalist, sees the ongoing shifts in her industry. She decides to take online courses on digital marketing, understanding that it's a growing field and her writing skills can be a valuable asset there.
   - ○ *Outcome:* When her media house faces challenges and starts downsizing, Maria smoothly transitions to a role in digital marketing, ensuring her income remains steady.

5. **Flexible Financial Goals:**
   - ○ *Scenario:* Raj has plans to buy a new home in the next five years. However, instead of fixating on a specific timeline, he remains flexible, understanding that

market conditions or his personal finances might
change.

○ *Outcome:* There's an economic recession three years
into his plan. Instead of taking a high-interest
mortgage during tough times, Raj decides to delay his
home purchase until he's in a more favorable financial
position.

Contingency planning is like building safety nets on the path to
financial freedom. These nets ensure that, should you stumble or face
challenges, you won't fall too far from your goals. By anticipating
potential obstacles and having provisions in place, individuals can
navigate the unpredictable waters of life with greater confidence and
resilience.

Philanthropy

Consider giving back to society through charitable donations.

Philanthropy involves making a difference in the world by devoting resources, often financial, to causes or initiatives that aim to improve the well-being of individuals, communities, or society at large. It's not merely about giving money; it's about making an impact. For many, philanthropy becomes an integral part of their financial journey as they achieve wealth and financial freedom. Not only does it provide an avenue for them to give back and make positive changes, but it also brings a sense of fulfillment and purpose.

EXAMPLES:

1. **Local Business Owner Supports Education:**
   - *Scenario:* Maria, a successful bakery owner, had grown up in a community where many couldn't afford higher education. Once she achieved financial stability, she decided to fund annual scholarships for deserving students from her community.
   - *Outcome:* Over the years, several students benefit from Maria's scholarships, getting access to education and opportunities they might not have otherwise had. In return, many of these students come back to serve the community, creating a cycle of positive impact.
2. **Monthly Donations:**

○ *Scenario:* Alex, a software engineer, hasn't reached millionaire status but has a stable income. He decides to allocate a small percentage of his monthly salary to a local food bank.

○ *Outcome:* Alex's consistent contributions help the food bank serve meals to those in need, ensuring that they can maintain their operations and serve a growing number of people, especially during economic downturns.

3. **Setting Up a Charitable Trust:**

○ *Scenario:* Ravi, after selling his tech startup, realizes a significant windfall. He's passionate about clean energy and decides to set up a charitable trust to fund research in renewable energy sources.

○ *Outcome:* The trust funds multiple research projects, one of which leads to a breakthrough in solar energy efficiency. This not only benefits the environment but also creates jobs and spurs further innovation in the sector.

4. **Microloans to Entrepreneurs:**

○ *Scenario:* Aisha, who has built a considerable portfolio from her investments, learns about a platform where she can provide microloans to entrepreneurs in developing countries.

○ *Outcome:* Aisha funds several small businesses, from craftswomen in Africa to farmers in South America. As these businesses grow, they uplift entire communities by providing local employment and improving living standards.

Philanthropy isn't just the domain of the ultra-rich. Anyone, at any financial level, can contribute to the betterment of society. The act of giving back, no matter the scale, can create ripple effects that benefit individuals and communities for generations. Beyond the tangible benefits for recipients, philanthropy also offers donors emotional and psychological rewards, reinforcing the idea that true wealth isn't just about personal gain but also about the positive impact one can make in the world.

PRINCIPLE 82

Adopt sustainable lifestyle

Minimise your carbon footprint to combat climate change.

Sustainable living refers to adopting a lifestyle that reduces an individual's or community's use of natural and personal resources. It's aimed at minimizing the negative impact one has on the world, particularly regarding climate change, ecosystem degradation, and resource depletion. By practicing sustainability, individuals not only contribute to environmental preservation but can also achieve financial freedom by reducing waste and unnecessary expenses.

EXAMPLES:

1. **Minimalist Living:**
   - *Scenario:* James, after reading about the benefits of minimalism, decides to downsize his home and possessions. He sells off what he doesn't need and moves to a smaller, energy-efficient apartment.
   - *Outcome:* James finds that he's saving a significant amount on utilities, maintenance, and other costs. Additionally, with fewer possessions, he feels less stressed and more focused. His reduced consumption also means a smaller carbon footprint.
2. **Growing Your Own Food:**
   - *Scenario:* A family in Oregon converts their backyard into a vegetable garden and starts composting.

    ○ *Outcome:* Not only do they reduce their grocery bills, but they also cut down on the carbon emissions associated with transporting food. The composting reduces their waste and replenishes the soil, creating a closed-loop system.

3. **Using Public Transport or Carpooling:**

    ○ *Scenario:* Maria, who used to drive to work every day, starts using the local train system.

    ○ *Outcome:* Maria saves on fuel, parking, and car maintenance costs. She also reduces her carbon emissions significantly. Over time, the money she saves allows her to invest more towards her financial goals.

4. **Adopting Renewable Energy:**

    ○ *Scenario:* The Smiths install solar panels on their home's roof.

    ○ *Outcome:* Their electricity bills drop, and in some months they even get a credit for supplying excess power back to the grid. The reduced reliance on non-renewable energy sources also diminishes their carbon footprint.

5. **Buying Second-hand or Sustainable Products:**

    ○ *Scenario:* Instead of buying fast fashion, Anika starts purchasing clothing from sustainable brands or second-hand shops.

    ○ *Outcome:* Anika ends up spending less on clothing annually, as she focuses on quality over quantity. Her choices also support industries that are environmentally friendly and reduce the waste and pollution associated with fast fashion.

6. **Reducing Water Waste:**

- ○ *Scenario:* A couple decides to install rainwater harvesting systems and low-flow fixtures in their home.
- ○ *Outcome:* Their water bill decreases, and they have an uninterrupted water supply, even in drier months. The reduced water consumption also means less strain on local water resources.

7. **Digital Nomad Lifestyle:**
   - ○ *Scenario:* John, a software developer, decides to adopt a digital nomad lifestyle. He travels to places where his daily expenses are lower and works remotely.
   - ○ *Outcome:* John significantly reduces his yearly expenses, leading to increased savings. By choosing locations with eco-friendly accommodations, he ensures his impact on the environment is minimal.

Sustainable living isn't just about helping the planet; it's also about re-evaluating our needs and making conscious decisions that benefit our finances and overall well-being. By reducing waste, being energy efficient, and supporting eco-friendly practices, one can effectively create a lifestyle that is beneficial for both the individual and the planet. Moreover, the money saved from sustainable practices can be redirected towards investments, further aiding in the journey toward financial freedom.

PRINCIPLE 83

Avoid bad habits

Avoid bad habits like gambling, smoking, alcoholism and drug abuse.

Maintaining bad habits can be both financially and physically draining, potentially leading to severe long-term consequences. These habits not only impose direct financial costs but also lead to potential health issues, increased medical expenses, and reduced work efficiency or lost job opportunities. Ultimately, indulging in such behaviours can impede one's journey towards achieving financial freedom.

EXAMPLES:

1. **Gambling:**
   - *Scenario:* Mark had a habit of frequenting casinos and betting on sports. He believed that he could make a quick buck and change his financial situation overnight.
   - *Outcome:* Over the years, Mark ended up losing a significant amount of his savings. His debts started piling up, and the stress made it difficult for him to focus on his job or find new sources of income.
2. **Smoking:**
   - *Scenario:* Lucy started smoking in her teenage years. On average, she smoked a pack a day, costing her $7.
   - *Outcome:* By the time Lucy turned 40, she had spent approximately $51,100 on cigarettes alone (not

accounting for inflation). Moreover, she started experiencing health problems, leading to high medical bills and frequent days off from work, further straining her finances.

3. **Alcoholism:**
   - ○ *Scenario:* Jake loved going out and drinking excessively with friends several times a week. Each night out would cost him around $100.
   - ○ *Outcome:* Over a year, Jake spent around $26,000 on alcohol and related expenses. As his drinking habit intensified, he faced potential job losses due to decreased productivity and attendance. His health deteriorated, incurring more medical expenses, and he also faced potential legal troubles from incidents like drunk driving.

4. **Drug Abuse:**
   - ○ *Scenario:* Aisha began experimenting with recreational drugs in college. As she grew older, her dependency on them increased, both in frequency and the types of drugs used.
   - ○ *Outcome:* Aisha's savings started dwindling as she spent more on procuring drugs. She faced difficulties at work and eventually lost her job. The health complications resulting from her drug use also led to considerable medical bills.

FINANCIAL IMPACT AND BROADER CONSIDERATIONS:

The immediate financial costs of these habits are evident, but there are broader ramifications too:

- **Healthcare Costs:** Bad habits often lead to health issues, resulting in higher medical bills and insurance premiums.

- ⊙ **Lost Opportunities:** Reduced productivity and frequent absences can result in missed promotions, wage cuts, or even job losses.
- ⊙ **Legal Implications:** Habits like excessive drinking or drug abuse can lead to legal troubles, which come with their own set of expenses including fines, legal fees, and potential loss of employment.
- ⊙ **Impact on Family:** These habits can strain familial relationships. It might lead to expenses related to counselling, or in extreme cases, divorce or child custody battles, both emotionally and financially taxing.
- ⊙ **Reduced Savings and Investments:** Money spent on these habits is money that's not being saved or invested for future growth. The opportunity cost over a lifetime can be substantial.

Avoiding detrimental habits is crucial for anyone looking to achieve financial freedom and overall well-being. The money saved by abstaining from these habits can be channelled towards investments, emergency funds, and other wealth-building tools, accelerating the journey towards financial stability and health.

Time is more valuable than money

You can get more money, but you cannot get more time.

This principle emphasizes that while you can always earn, invest, and recoup money, time, once spent, can never be reclaimed. This understanding can greatly influence decisions, especially when one is trying to achieve financial freedom and overall well-being.

1. Compound Interest:

One of the most straightforward examples of this concept in the realm of finance is the power of compound interest. The earlier you start investing, the more time your money has to grow, thanks to the interest on the interest (compounding). For instance, if Person A starts investing $200 a month at age 25 at an 8% return rate, and Person B starts investing the same amount at age 35 (with the same return rate), by age 60, Person A will have significantly more money than Person B, even though they both invested the same amount monthly.

2. Career Choices:

Consider two individuals: Person X spends several years in higher education and skill acquisition, incurring student debt but eventually securing a high-paying job. Person Y starts working straight out of high school in a job with limited growth prospects. Although Person Y may initially earn more and have no student loans, Person X, in the long run, will likely outpace in earnings and career growth, illustrating that the investment of time (in education) can have long-term financial benefits.

3. Health and Well-being:

Time spent on self-care, regular health check-ups, and exercise might seem like a 'cost' or 'time not spent earning money'. However, in the long run, maintaining good health can save substantial amounts of money on medical bills, ensure longevity in one's career, and increase overall productivity.

4. Learning and Skill Acquisition:

Investing time in continuous learning can lead to better job opportunities, side hustles, or investment insights. For example, spending time understanding the stock market or real estate trends might initially seem like time not directly spent earning. However, this knowledge can translate to substantial financial gains in the future.

5. Quality vs. Quantity:

Instead of working endless hours to earn more, focusing on efficiency, work quality, and achieving a work-life balance can lead to better job satisfaction, promotions, or even opportunities to start a business. Overworking might provide immediate financial gains but can lead to burnout, health issues, and decreased productivity over time.

Recognizing the irreplaceable value of time can transform how one approaches finances, career decisions, personal health, and relationships. By respecting time's intrinsic value and understanding its potential long-term benefits, individuals can make choices that not only lead to financial freedom but also a rich, fulfilling life.

Trust yourself, know yourself, and don't sell yourself short.

The world will value you at your own estimated value.

The world will value you at your own estimated value" encapsulates the essence of self-worth, confidence, and self-awareness, especially in contexts like personal growth, career, and wealth creation. Essentially, this suggests that how you perceive and present yourself plays a significant role in determining how the world responds to you. Here's a deeper dive into the statement with relevant examples:

1. The Job Market:

Example: Consider two candidates, Alice and Bob, interviewing for the same position. Both have similar qualifications, but Alice undersells her achievements and capabilities, while Bob confidently communicates his worth and backs it up with examples. Bob is more likely to be offered a higher salary because he effectively communicated his value.

Interpretation: When you undervalue your skills or contributions, you might settle for less than what you're worth. On the contrary, a clear understanding and communication of your worth often translate to better compensation and respect in professional settings.

2. Business and Entrepreneurship:

Example: Sarah has a start-up idea but is hesitant because she's unsure about her capabilities. She downplays her concept to potential investors. On the other hand, John, with a similar idea, fully believes in his vision, pitches it with confidence, and secures funding.

Interpretation: Trusting in your abilities and the value of your ideas is crucial, especially in the entrepreneurial world. Investors and partners are more likely to back someone who exudes confidence and belief in their concept.

3. Investment and Financial Decisions:

Example: Mark comes across a potential investment opportunity. He's done his research, and all indicators suggest it's a good bet. However, due to a lack of self-confidence, he hesitates and misses out. Jane, with the same information, trusts her judgment, invests, and reaps substantial returns.

Interpretation: Trusting yourself is especially crucial when making financial decisions. While it's essential to be informed and cautious, second-guessing valid decisions due to a lack of self-confidence can lead to missed opportunities.

4. Personal Growth and Education:

Example: Priya, unsure about her capabilities, avoids taking challenging courses or projects that could advance her career. In contrast, Ravi, recognizing his potential and areas of growth, takes on these challenges and uses them as stepping stones for advancement.

Interpretation: Knowing and pushing your limits can lead to substantial personal and professional growth. By avoiding challenges due to self-doubt, you might be stunting your potential.

Your self-worth and self-perception have a tangible impact on your journey towards financial freedom and overall success. By recognizing your value and not being afraid to assert it, you set a precedent for how others perceive and interact with you. Remember, the world often mirrors back the image you project. If you showcase confidence, trust, and self-worth, the world is more likely to respond in kind.

Priority Management: Aligning Your Schedule with Your Goals

The key is not to prioritise what's on your schedule, but to schedule your priorities,

This principle emphasizes the importance of proactive planning and setting clear goals rather than being reactive to the myriad tasks and requests that come our way. This statement underscores the value of time management, focus, and the alignment of actions with personal and financial goals. Let's delve deeper into this concept with relevant examples:

1. Personal Savings and Investments:

Example: Jake receives his pay check at the beginning of the month. Rather than setting aside a portion for savings and investment first, he pays his bills, spends on leisure, and only saves what's left over. Often, he finds that he's left with very little to save. On the other hand, Maria, as soon as she receives her pay check, immediately transfers a fixed percentage into her savings and investment accounts. She's making saving a priority.

Interpretation: By scheduling the priority of saving first, Maria ensures she's steadily building her wealth and moving closer to financial freedom. Jake, in contrast, is leaving his financial growth to chance.

2. Entrepreneurship and Business:

Example: David owns a startup. Every day, he finds himself bogged down by small administrative tasks, meetings, and operational chores. He rarely finds time for strategic planning or networking, which are crucial for his business's growth. Conversely, Natasha, another entrepreneur, begins her week by blocking out periods in her schedule dedicated solely to growth activities like strategy sessions, mentor meetings, and client outreach.

Interpretation: By scheduling her key priorities, Natasha ensures that she dedicates time to the tasks that have the most significant potential impact on her business's future.

3. Continuing Education and Skill Development:

Example: Carlos wants to improve his financial literacy to make better investment choices. But his week always feels packed, and he tells himself he'll start studying "when he gets some free time." Amelia, with a similar goal, designates every Saturday morning to read a new financial book or take an online course.

Interpretation: Amelia has scheduled her priority of learning, ensuring she consistently works towards her goal. In contrast, Carlos, by waiting for a free slot in his busy schedule, might never get around to it.

4. Debt Repayment:

Example: Sean has multiple debts: credit card bills, a car loan, and a personal loan. Rather than having a structured repayment plan, he pays off whatever bill seems most urgent at the moment. Leah, in a similar debt situation, outlines a clear debt repayment strategy prioritizing high-interest debts and schedules monthly payments accordingly.

Interpretation: By scheduling her debt repayment priorities, Leah ensures she tackles her debt in the most cost-effective manner, saving on interest over time.

The essence of the statement is about intentionality. In the realm of financial freedom and wealth creation, those who act deliberately and set clear priorities are more likely to succeed. It's about deciding what's truly important for your financial future and ensuring those tasks are given precedence in your life.

Fear kills more dreams than failure ever will

This principle emphasizes the paralysing effect that fear can have on individuals, often preventing them from even attempting to pursue their goals. While failure is a natural part of growth and can offer lessons, fear can completely stop someone from taking any action at all. When related to wealth creation and achieving financial freedom, this sentiment underscores the idea that inaction born out of fear can be more detrimental than making mistakes along the journey. Let's explore this further with some examples:

1. Investing in the Stock Market:

Example: Jasmine has saved a substantial amount over the years. She's heard about the potential returns in the stock market but is too scared of losing her hard-earned money, so she never invests. On the other hand, Alex, despite initial reservations, decides to start investing. He faces some losses early on, but he learns from his mistakes, adjusts his strategy, and eventually sees significant returns.

Interpretation: While Alex encountered failure, he used it as a learning opportunity and ultimately benefited. Jasmine's fear prevented her from even starting, potentially missing out on substantial financial growth.

2. Starting a Business:

Example: Carlos has a fantastic idea for a startup and has even drafted a business plan. However, the fear of failing and the potential financial risks make him hesitant to take the plunge. Meanwhile, Rita, with a similar idea, decides to start her own business. Though she faces numerous challenges and even contemplates shutting down at one point, she perseveres, pivots her business model, and eventually finds success.

Interpretation: Rita's willingness to face failure and adapt allowed her to achieve her dream, while Carlos's fear kept his dream confined to paper.

3. Real Estate Investment:

Example: Sophia comes across an opportunity to invest in a property that's predicted to appreciate significantly. However, she's paralysed by the fear of the property market crashing or making a bad decision. Michael, despite similar concerns, conducts thorough research and decides to buy a property. Even when the property market temporarily dips, he holds on, and in a decade, the value of his property doubles.

Interpretation: While Michael took a calculated risk and faced temporary setbacks, he benefitted in the long run. Sophia's fear prevented her from capitalizing on a lucrative opportunity.

4. Personal Development and Networking:

Example: Liam wants to improve his financial literacy and considers attending a financial workshop. However, the fear of feeling out of place or not understanding the content holds him back. In contrast, Naomi, with the same reservations, attends the workshop, asks questions, and even makes some valuable connections that later help her in her financial journey.

Interpretation: Naomi's willingness to step out of her comfort zone and face potential embarrassment led to personal growth and opportunities. Liam's fear kept him from acquiring knowledge and connections.

The essence of the statement is about the significance of confronting fear and taking action. In the context of financial freedom and wealth creation, avoiding risks altogether due to fear can result in missed opportunities and stagnation. While failure might pose challenges, it also offers invaluable lessons and growth opportunities, whereas fear-induced inaction ensures neither growth nor lessons.

PRINCIPLE 88

Life Lessons through Adversity

A hungry stomach, an empty wallet and a broken hear can teach you the best of life lessons.

This alludes to the idea that adversity and hardship, while painful, often lead to profound personal growth, clarity, and resilience. These challenges push individuals to introspect, reevaluate their priorities, and discover strengths they didn't know they had. When it comes to wealth creation and achieving financial freedom, such life lessons can guide more informed, mindful, and resilient decisions in the future. Let's delve deeper into this concept using the three components of the statement:

1. A Hungry Stomach:

Meaning: Facing extreme necessity or dire situations, such as literal hunger or a deep need for something in life.

Financial Example: After losing her job, Maria struggled to make ends meet, often skipping meals to ensure her children ate. This period taught her the importance of an emergency fund, the value of frugality, and the skills to find alternative income sources. When she finally secured another job, Maria became a diligent saver and investor, ensuring she wouldn't be in such a position again.

Lesson: Experiencing scarcity can teach the importance of preparation, resilience, and adaptability in financial journeys.

2. An Empty Wallet:

Meaning: Facing financial hardship or understanding the implications of poor financial decisions.

Financial Example: Sam, once a lavish spender with no concept of saving, found himself burdened with debt and no savings when an economic downturn hit. This experience was a wake-up call. Sam sought financial education, learned budgeting, and worked his way out of debt. From then on, he made it a priority to save, invest, and live below his means.

Lesson: Financial adversity can underscore the importance of financial literacy, discipline, and the need to balance present desires with future security.

3. A Broken Heart:

Meaning: Emotional pain, disappointment, or betrayal, which can lead to introspection and personal growth.

Financial Example: Alex entered into a business partnership with a close friend. Over time, however, it became clear that his friend was mismanaging funds, leading to a business breakdown and loss of their friendship. The emotional and financial toll taught Alex to separate emotions from business, conduct thorough background checks, and implement checks and balances in future ventures.

Lesson: Emotional setbacks, especially when intertwined with financial matters, highlight the importance of due diligence, boundaries, and the necessity of not letting emotions cloud judgment.

While no one seeks out hardship, it's undeniable that challenging experiences often come with valuable lessons. In the realm of financial freedom and wealth-building, such lessons can form the foundation for smarter, more informed decisions, emphasizing the idea that while pain is sometimes unavoidable, growth from that pain is a choice.

Enduring Challenges with a Strong Mindset

Strong minds suffer without complaining. Weak minds complain without suffering .

This touches upon the idea of resilience, mental fortitude, and perspective. It suggests that individuals with mental strength often endure challenges silently, pushing through adversity without vocalizing their distress, while those who lack this resilience might complain even in the absence of significant hardships. In the context of wealth creation and financial freedom, this mindset can play a pivotal role. Let's understand this using financial examples:

1. Strong Minds Suffer Without Complaining:

People with a resilient and determined mindset face challenges head-on, maintaining a positive attitude and refraining from excessive complaining, even when faced with genuine hardships.

Financial Example: Jane had always dreamt of owning a bakery. She invested a significant portion of her savings to start one. Unfortunately, a series of unforeseen events, including a market downturn and a location issue, led to severe financial strain in the first year. Rather than lamenting her situation or playing the victim, Jane silently sought solutions, worked extra hours, learned from her mistakes, and slowly steered her business back on track. She didn't vocalize her troubles excessively but focused on actions.

Those with strong minds view challenges as temporary setbacks, learning opportunities, or stepping stones to future success. They believe in finding solutions rather than dwelling on problems, and this approach is instrumental in the path to wealth and financial freedom.

2. Weak Minds Complain Without Suffering:

Meaning: Some individuals may exhibit a tendency to complain or showcase a negative perspective even when their challenges aren't particularly severe or even present.

Financial Example: Tom had a stable job and no significant financial burdens. However, he constantly complained about not having enough, the unfairness of the economy, or the successes of his peers, often without taking initiatives to improve his financial knowledge or make new investments. His complaints were more a result of a fixed mindset than any actual financial suffering.

Lesson: Merely complaining without actionable efforts, especially in the absence of genuine hardships, can hinder financial growth. It can lead to missed opportunities, inaction, and a negative mindset that's counterproductive to wealth creation.

The journey to financial freedom and wealth creation is as much about mindset as it is about monetary strategies. Embracing resilience, learning from challenges, and maintaining a proactive, solution-focused attitude can be the difference between financial success and stagnation. The way one responds to setbacks—whether with actionable solutions or mere complaints—can dictate the trajectory of their financial journey.

What comes easy, won't last.
What lasts, won't come easy

Enduring success and value often require effort, persistence, and time. Quick wins or shortcuts might offer immediate gratification, but they are usually not sustainable in the long run. In contrast, things that are built over time with dedication are more likely to have a lasting impact. Within the framework of wealth creation and financial freedom, this wisdom has profound implications. Let's delve deeper with some examples:

1. What comes easy, won't last:

Meaning: Quick financial gains or shortcuts might be tempting, but they often come with risks and might not provide long-term benefits.

Financial Example: Jake hears about a "get-rich-quick" scheme from a friend. He invests a significant portion of his savings, hoping for fast returns. Initially, he sees some profit, but soon, the scheme collapses, and Jake loses most of his investment. The easy money he thought he was earning disappeared just as quickly.

Lesson: Financial ventures that promise high returns in a short period, without a sound basis, are often risky. Sustainable wealth is rarely built overnight. Quick, easy solutions might provide short-lived success, but they can also lead to significant losses.

2. What lasts, won't come easy:

Meaning: Achieving enduring success, especially in the realm of finance, requires patience, informed decisions, and consistent effort.

Financial Example: Maria started investing a small portion of her salary in a diversified portfolio when she was 25. The investments didn't make her rich quickly, and there were times when the market was down, testing her patience. However, she held on, kept herself informed, and continued her investments. By the time she retired, her consistent, informed approach had yielded a substantial nest egg, providing her financial freedom in her golden years.

Lesson: Long-term investments, continuous learning, and patience in the financial world often leads to compound growth and sustainable wealth. While the journey may have challenges and might not offer instant gratification, the end result is often worth the effort and wait.

In the quest for financial freedom and wealth, it's crucial to recognize the value of perseverance, informed decision-making, and long-term planning. While shortcuts and easy wins can be tempting, they may not provide lasting value. On the other hand, consistent effort, even if it feels slow or challenging, is more likely to result in sustainable success and enduring financial security.

Losers stop when they fail, Winners fail till they succeed

This principle emphasises the power of perseverance and resilience in the face of adversity, suggesting that success is not necessarily about avoiding failure but about how one responds to it.

1. **Mindset:** At its core, this statement underscores the difference between a fixed mindset and a growth mindset. Those with a fixed mindset believe their abilities are static, while those with a growth mindset see challenges as opportunities to grow and learn. In the context of financial freedom and wealth creation, adopting a growth mindset means viewing financial setbacks not as ultimate failures but as learning experiences.

   Example: If an individual's investment in a startup doesn't yield expected returns, rather than swearing off future investments, they might assess what went wrong, educate themselves further, and make a more informed investment next time.

2. **The Role of Persistence:** Financial freedom often doesn't happen overnight. It requires planning, discipline, and, most importantly, the persistence to stay the course even when things look bleak.

   Example: Consider the numerous stories of successful entrepreneurs who faced bankruptcy or significant financial loss before eventually making it big. Walt Disney, for instance, was fired from a newspaper for "lacking imagination." His first animation company went bankrupt. Instead of giving up, he kept experimenting and iterating until he founded the Disney empire we know today.

3. **Risk and Reward:** Building substantial wealth often involves taking calculated risks. Those who fear failure might avoid risks entirely and, in doing so, also miss out on potential rewards.

   Example: An individual might avoid investing in the stock market because they're afraid of potential losses. However, by staying out, they also miss out on potential gains. On the other hand, someone who understands that markets have ups and downs might ride out short-term losses, adjusting their strategy as needed until they see returns on their investments.

4. **Learning from Mistakes:** The road to financial freedom will almost certainly include some missteps. However, those committed to achieving their goals will use these mistakes as learning opportunities.

   Example: An individual might splurge on a luxury car, only to realize later that they've hampered their ability to save or invest. Instead of repeating this mistake, they might then choose to live below their means, prioritizing savings and investments over short-term pleasures.

The journey to financial freedom and wealth creation is seldom a straight path. It's marked by challenges, setbacks, and failures. The key is not to avoid these challenges but to learn from them, iterate, and keep pushing forward until you reach your desired goals.

Don't talk, ACT. Don't say, SHOW. Don't promise, Prove

These statements highlight the importance of taking action over merely voicing intentions. In the realm of financial freedom and wealth creation, actions speak louder than words, and results often serve as the most genuine reflection of commitment and capability.

1. **Don't talk, ACT:** It's easy to discuss desires, intentions, or plans, but the real progress towards financial freedom starts when you initiate action.

    Example: Tom always talks about the importance of saving money and investing wisely. However, he spends lavishly without setting aside any funds for savings or investments. On the other hand, Jerry, who is less vocal about his financial strategies, regularly allocates a portion of his income to a diversified investment portfolio. Over time, Jerry's actions yield substantial returns, while Tom's mere talk doesn't translate into any tangible financial growth.

2. **Don't say, SHOW:** Expressing aspirations or plans is the first step, but showcasing tangible results or progress is what earns respect and trust, especially in financial matters.

    Example: Lisa constantly speaks about her plans to buy a house. She discusses different properties, locations, and interior design ideas but never actually makes any move towards purchasing a property. In contrast, Amy quietly researches the real estate market, consults with a realtor, saves diligently for a down payment, and eventually buys her dream home. Amy's actions, rather than mere words, demonstrate her commitment and capability.

3. **Don't promise, prove:** Promising future success or intent can set expectations, but delivering on those promises is what truly counts, especially when it comes to financial commitments.

   Example: David, an entrepreneur, promises his investors high returns on their investments in his startup. While his intentions might be genuine, unless he can demonstrate growth, profitability, and a return on investment, his promises remain hollow. On the other hand, Sarah, another entrepreneur, might secure fewer investors initially but focuses on steadily growing her business. As she starts to deliver consistent returns, she not only proves her reliability to her current investors but also attracts more in the future.

In the context of achieving financial freedom, these statements underscore the importance of discipline, commitment, and execution. Talking about financial goals is the easy part; acting on them, demonstrating progress, and delivering on promises are the aspects that truly drive success.

PRINCIPLE 93

Selective Alliances

Intelligent people tend to have less friends than average person. The smarter you are the more selective you become and that's ok.

The smarter you are the more selective you become about friends and that's OK" can be interpreted in various ways. When applied to the realm of personal finance and wealth-building, it accentuates the principles of discernment, focused effort, and the significance of quality over quantity. Let's explore this sentiment in the context of wealth and financial freedom:

1. **Value of Depth Over Breadth**:
    ○   **Example**: Just as an intelligent individual may prefer a few deep, insightful conversations over many surface-level interactions, a savvy investor might value deep knowledge in a specific sector over a superficial understanding of many. This depth can lead to more informed decisions and, potentially, better investment outcomes.
2. **Importance of Quality Connections**:
    ○   **Example**: In the business world, it's often not about how many connections you have but the quality of those connections. An entrepreneur might only need a few but highly influential backers or mentors to succeed, rather than hundreds of less impactful supporters. Likewise, a smart individual understands

that nurturing a few genuine relationships can be more fulfilling and beneficial than trying to maintain many shallow ones.

3. **Guarding One's Time and Resources:**
   - ○ **Example:** Time is a finite resource, often deemed more precious than money because it can't be replenished. By being selective with whom they spend time, intelligent individuals ensure they invest their hours in meaningful ways. Financially speaking, this can be likened to a discerning investor who carefully chooses where to allocate their funds, ensuring each dollar is purposefully invested.

4. **Reduced Exposure to Financial Peer Pressure:**
   - ○ **Example:** One of the pitfalls many faces is lifestyle inflation and spending to keep up with peers. By having fewer but more meaningful friendships, one may feel less pressure to spend on unnecessary extravagances or engage in financial behaviours misaligned with their goals. An individual who is selective about their friendships might be surrounded by supportive people who understand and respect their financial journey and choices.

5. **The Principle of Focus:**
   - ○ **Example:** A common saying in the financial world is "Jack of all trades, master of none." An investor spreading themselves too thin might miss out on significant opportunities. Similarly, by focusing on a few critical friendships, individuals can nurture these relationships to be strong, supportive, and lasting, providing a stable emotional and perhaps even financial network.

In summary, the statement underscores the merits of selectivity, emphasizing that quality often trumps quantity, especially in the context of relationships and personal growth. Translated to the domain of financial freedom, it's a reminder that judicious choices, whether in friendships or finances, can lead to more profound, more lasting rewards. It's a nod to the idea that in both life and money, more isn't always better; better is better.

PRINCIPLE 94

The biggest asset in the world is your mindset

This reflects the idea that the way one thinks, perceives, and approaches situations can either unlock immense potential or become a limiting factor. In the context of wealth and achieving financial freedom, a person's mindset can determine their financial outcomes. Here's a deeper exploration with some examples:

1. **Growth vs. Fixed Mindset**:
   - ○ **Example**: Two people receive the same salary. One believes they're stuck at their income level and doesn't seek ways to increase it. The other believes in self-improvement and constantly seeks opportunities for side hustles or investments. Over time, the person with the growth mindset likely accumulates more wealth.

2. **Abundance vs. Scarcity Mentality**:
   - ○ **Example**: A person with an abundance mentality believes there are plenty of opportunities to generate wealth and is optimistic about financial future. They might invest in a promising stock or start a business, believing in the potential for success. Conversely, someone with a scarcity mentality might hoard money or avoid investments due to fear of loss.

3. **Long-Term Thinking**:

○ **Example**: Consider two investors. One is always chasing the next "hot stock" or trend, jumping from one investment to the next, while the other has a long-term perspective, investing in solid assets and waiting patiently for compounding to work its magic. Historically, long-term investments often outperform short-term speculative ones.

4. **Reactive vs. Proactive Mindset**:

○ **Example**: A proactive individual creates an emergency fund, anticipating potential financial downturns. A reactive individual, however, waits until a crisis hits and then struggles to manage, often incurring debts or selling assets at a loss.

5. **Learning from Failures**:

○ **Example**: An entrepreneur with a positive mindset treats a business failure as a lesson, learning from mistakes, pivoting, and trying again. On the other hand, someone with a negative mindset might view such a failure as a sign they're not cut out for business, potentially missing out on future successful ventures.

6. **Value Perception**:

○ **Example**: While some might see spending on education or personal development as an expense, others with a growth mindset see it as an investment. This perspective can lead to better career opportunities and income potentials.

7. **Flexibility and Adaptability**:

○ **Example**: In rapidly changing markets, those with adaptable mindsets, who are willing to learn and shift strategies, often fare better than those rigid in their approaches. For instance, investors who adapted to the rise of tech and renewable energy sectors have seen significant returns in recent years.

Your mindset plays a pivotal role in your financial journey. While external factors matter, it's often your reactions, beliefs, and attitudes towards these circumstances that determine success. As the saying goes, "It's not what happens to you, but how you react to it that matters." In the world of finance, this couldn't be truer. By cultivating a positive, growth-oriented mindset, individuals can better navigate the complexities of wealth generation and financial freedom.

PRINCIPLE 95

Don't criticize, condemn or complain.

These statements emphasize the importance of understanding human nature, especially when it comes to interpersonal relationships and leadership. The overarching message is about the power of positivity, encouragement, and the importance of avoiding criticism. Here's a deeper exploration of these statements in the context of wealth and financial freedom:

1. **Don't criticize, condemn or complain**:
   - ○ **Elaboration**: Negative attitudes or behaviours like criticizing, condemning, or complaining don't foster growth.
   - ○ **Example**: In a business setting, a leader who constantly complains or criticizes employees can demoralize the team, leading to reduced productivity and potentially impacting profitability.
2. **Strong people don't put others down. They lift them up**:
   - ○ **Elaboration**: True strength is showcased not in demeaning others but in empowering and uplifting them.
   - ○ **Example**: A successful entrepreneur mentors a young aspirant, providing guidance and resources to help them start their own venture, rather than viewing them as competition.

3. **Ninety-nine times out of a hundred, people don't criticize themselves for anything, no matter how wrong it may be:**
   - ○ **Elaboration**: People often find it difficult to self-reflect and accept their mistakes.
   - ○ **Example**: An investor blames market volatility for a failed investment, rather than acknowledging a lack of research on their part.

4. **Criticism is dangerous:**
   - ○ **Elaboration**: Direct criticism can lead to defensiveness and resentment, hindering constructive discussions.
   - ○ **Example**: Telling a business partner their idea is terrible might sour the relationship, whereas constructive feedback could lead to refining the idea into something successful.

5. **Animals rewarded for good behaviour learn more rapidly:**
   - ○ **Elaboration**: Positive reinforcement is a powerful tool for growth and learning.
   - ○ **Example**: A sales team given bonuses and recognition for meeting targets is likely more motivated and efficient than one that's reprimanded for every missed sale.

6. **By criticizing, we do not make lasting changes:**
   - ○ **Elaboration**: Real, lasting change comes from understanding, collaboration, and positive reinforcement, not from pointing out faults.
   - ○ **Example**: Continuously pointing out an employee's mistakes without providing solutions may lead them to repeat errors or even resign, instead of improving.

7. **We are all like that:**

- ○ **Elaboration**: It's human nature to shift blame, but recognizing this trait can lead to personal growth.
- ○ **Example**: An individual overspending their budget blames unexpected expenses, but upon reflection, realizes impulse purchases were the real issue.

8. **We are dealing with creatures of emotion**:
    - ○ **Elaboration**: People are driven by emotions, pride, and vanity, which can influence financial and investment decisions.
    - ○ **Example**: An individual might purchase a luxury car to elevate their social status rather than investing that money.

In essence, the way we interact with others, especially in positions of leadership or influence, has profound effects on our journey towards wealth and financial freedom. Positive interactions and understanding human nature can lead to collaborations, growth opportunities, and a more harmonious path to success.

Strong people don't put others down. They lift them up

emphasizes the true nature of strength, which is characterized not by dominating or belittling others but by empowering and aiding them. This idea has significant implications for personal development, leadership, and financial success.

1. **Leadership and Mentorship**:
   - ○ Genuine strength is displayed when individuals use their knowledge, resources, or position to assist others in achieving their goals. In the realm of wealth creation, effective leaders recognize the potential in others and foster an environment of mutual growth.
   - ○ *Example*: A successful entrepreneur might establish a mentorship program for young entrepreneurs. By sharing their knowledge and resources, they not only help budding entrepreneurs thrive but also enrich the business ecosystem, potentially creating beneficial partnerships for the future.

2. **Team Dynamics and Business Growth**:
   - ○ Companies or teams thrive when members uplift each other, fostering an environment of collaboration rather than competition.

○ *Example*: In a startup, when one department faces challenges, strong leaders from other departments will offer support and resources to help overcome the obstacle. This collective effort can expedite the company's growth trajectory, leading to quicker profitability and success.

3. **Investment in People**:

    ○ Investing in people—be it through education, training, or simply providing opportunities—often yields a high return in terms of loyalty, productivity, and innovation.

    ○ *Example*: A business owner who funds the education of a promising employee might see returns in the form of increased innovation or efficiency in their business operations.

4. **Networking and Collaborations**:

    ○ By uplifting others, strong individuals often foster a network of goodwill and collaboration. This network can be leveraged for business opportunities, partnerships, and investments.

    ○ *Example*: An investor who helps a struggling but promising company by offering strategic advice, rather than just capital, may find that as the company grows, they're offered favourable terms for future collaborations.

5. **Personal Brand and Reputation**:

    ○ Those who consistently uplift others often garner respect and trust in their community or industry. This positive reputation can lead to more opportunities for growth and wealth creation.

○ *Example*: A real estate mogul known for investing in community development and providing affordable housing might find that they have a stronger community brand, leading to more lucrative deals and partnerships.

In the journey towards wealth and financial freedom, the relationships and reputations we build are invaluable. True strength, in this journey, isn't showcased by how many people one can overshadow but by how many one can help rise.

Proactive Steps Toward Progress and achievement

Proactively pursue your goals, for inaction guarantees neither progress nor attainment.

this principle emphasizes proactive behaviour, the significance of persistence, and the courage to embrace change. In the context of creating wealth and achieving financial freedom, these rules can provide a roadmap for success.

1. **If you don't go after what you want, you'll never have it.**
    ○ **Ambition and Vision**: For one to achieve any significant milestone, be it wealth creation or otherwise, one must first have a clear goal in mind. Without a target, efforts can become scattered and inefficient.
    ○ **Example**: Consider an individual who dreams of owning a successful e-commerce business. Instead of just daydreaming, they start by researching market trends, understanding consumer needs, and learning about supply chain management. By actively pursuing their ambition, they're much more likely to make it a reality.

2. **If you don't ask, the answer is always no.**

   ○ **Risk-taking and Initiative**: Success often requires stepping out of one's comfort zone and taking risks. This might mean asking for investments, seeking mentorship, or negotiating deals. Fear of rejection shouldn't deter one from taking such steps because not asking guarantees denial.

   ○ **Example**: Imagine a young entrepreneur looking for funding to expand their startup. They identify a potential investor but are hesitant to approach due to fear of rejection. If they never muster the courage to pitch their business idea, they've essentially sealed their own fate to a "no." However, by simply asking, they open up the possibility of securing crucial funding.

3. **If you don't step forward, you're always in the same place.**

   ○ **Growth and Progress**: To advance in any sphere of life, one must be willing to move, adapt, and evolve. This might mean learning new skills, exploring unfamiliar territories, or changing outdated mindsets. Stagnation can be the biggest enemy of progress, especially in the ever-evolving world of finance and business.

   ○ **Example**: A stock market investor who's been using the same strategy for years might find their returns dwindling due to changing market dynamics. If they resist adapting to newer trading strategies or diversifying their portfolio, they risk diminishing returns. On the contrary, by staying updated and being open to new methodologies, they stand a better chance at consistent growth.

These rules emphasize a proactive and resilient approach to life and business. They underscore the necessity of ambition, the courage to take risks, and the willingness to grow—all crucial ingredients in the recipe for wealth and financial freedom.

Consistent actions evolve into habits that shape our financial lifestyle

Do it once = Action
Do it twice = Repetition
Do it few times = Behaviour
Do it multiple months = Habit
Do it for a year = Life style

1. **Do it once = Action**: Taking the initiative to start a task or change a behaviour is the primary step. For instance, if you've never created a budget before, the mere act of drafting one is an action. This is where change begins.
   Example: Lucy decides to invest in stocks. She does her research and buys shares in a promising company. It's a single action toward growing her wealth.

2. **Do it twice = Repetition**: Doing something repeatedly reinforces it. If you save money regularly or consistently avoid unnecessary expenses, you start building a pattern.
   Example: Every month, Lucy sets aside a portion of her income to buy more shares, reinforcing her initial action.

3. **Do it few times = Behaviour**: A repeated action becomes behaviour. If every time you receive a bonus, you invest half of it, it's no longer a one-off action but a behaviour.

Example: Over time, Lucy gets comfortable with stock trading and starts diversifying, investing in different sectors and regularly monitoring her portfolio's performance.

4. **Do it multiple months = Habit**: When you practice a behaviour consistently over an extended period, it becomes a habit. This could be anything from saving a certain percentage of your salary each month to consistently investing in your retirement fund.

    Example: Lucy now automatically diverts a set amount into her stock portfolio every month without even thinking about it. It's become second nature to her.

5. **Do it for a year = Lifestyle**: Over an extended period, these habits merge into your daily life and dictate how you live. If you've habitually lived below your means, invested wisely, and avoided debt, you'll find that this financially prudent approach has become your lifestyle.

    Example: A year down the line, Lucy isn't just an occasional stock investor. She's a seasoned investor with a diversified portfolio, an emergency fund, and a strict budget she adheres to. Her initial action has now shaped her entire financial lifestyle.

The occasional splurge or one-time investment won't drastically alter your financial trajectory. However, consistent actions—whether they're saving, investing, or being frugal—shape your financial future. It emphasizes the importance of regularity and consistency in building wealth and achieving financial freedom.

In essence, while a single action can initiate change, it's the repeated, consistent actions that lead to lasting results in one's financial journey. It's the habits and behaviours that we inculcate over time that truly dictate our financial health and our journey towards financial freedom.

Pay attention to your gut feelings

Trust your intuition; if an opportunity doesn't feel right, avoid it.

Our intuitive responses, or "gut feelings," are the culmination of past experiences, observations, and subconscious awareness. Often, our intuition operates in the background, nudging us towards or away from certain decisions. In the world of finance and investments, where data and analysis are king, one might assume that there's no room for intuition. Yet, many of the most successful investors and financial experts will attest to the importance of gut feelings in their decision-making processes.

EXAMPLES:

1. **Real Estate Investments:**
   - *Scenario:* John, a seasoned real estate investor, is looking to buy a new property. He's presented with two properties that on paper seem to offer similar returns. neighbourhood, despite its However, when visiting one of the properties, he gets an uneasy feeling about the current reputation.
   - *Outcome:* John decides to trust his gut and chooses the other property. A year later, the neighbourhood of the first property starts facing increased crime rates, which depreciates property values. John's intuition saved him from a bad investment.

2. **Stock Market Investments:**

   ○ *Scenario:* Sarah, a stock market enthusiast, is researching new stocks to invest in. She comes across a tech startup with excellent projections and promising reviews. However, something about the company's leadership doesn't sit right with her, even though they have good credentials.

   ○ *Outcome:* Sarah chooses not to invest. A few months down the line, the startup faces internal management issues, leading to a significant drop in stock prices. Sarah's gut feeling saved her from a potential loss.

3. **Entrepreneurship:**

   ○ *Scenario:* Raj is a budding entrepreneur and gets an opportunity to partner with a well-established firm. While the deal seems profitable, he feels that the values of the firm don't align with his own.

   ○ *Outcome:* Raj decides to decline the partnership and pursue his venture independently. Later, he learns that the firm had a history of unethical practices which could have tarnished his brand's reputation.

4. **Personal Savings:**

   ○ *Scenario:* Alice has saved a considerable amount of money and is considering putting it into a high-yield savings scheme offered by a relatively new bank. Despite the attractive interest rates, she feels sceptical about the bank's longevity.

   ○ *Outcome:* Alice opts for a more established bank with slightly lower interest rates. A year later, the new bank goes under due to mismanagement, and many lose their savings. Alice's intuitive caution preserved her hard-earned money.

In the journey to financial freedom, while it's crucial to make decisions based on research, analysis, and logic, it's equally vital not to ignore intuitive signals. The subconscious mind picks up on patterns and inconsistencies that the conscious mind might overlook. By tuning into and respecting these intuitive signals, one can avoid potential pitfalls and make choices that align more closely with long-term financial goals.

Recognizing Valuable Allies in Every Phase of Life

There are rare people who will show up at the right time, help you through hard times and stay into your best times. Those are the keepers.

Achieving wealth, financial freedom, and overall success often requires more than just individual effort. The journey is riddled with challenges, uncertainties, and crucial decision points. In these moments, the presence of reliable and steadfast people can be the game-changer. Their timely support, advice, or even just their belief in you can re-energize your efforts and offer clarity.

EXAMPLES:

1. **Mentors in the Professional World:** Think of a young professional navigating the corporate ladder or the startup ecosystem. A mentor who provides guidance during the early days, offers connections, and even helps steer through career roadblocks can be invaluable. For instance, a mentor might connect an individual with an investor or advise against a potentially bad business decision.

2. **Supportive Spouse or Partner:** For many successful entrepreneurs or professionals, there's often a supportive spouse or partner behind the scenes. This person offers

emotional support, understands the sacrifices being made, and sometimes might even provide financial backing. Consider the story of Jeff Bezos, whose wife, MacKenzie, supported the idea of Amazon and even did the company's accounting in its initial days.

3. **Loyal Business Partners:** Successful ventures often have at their core a team of co-founders or early employees who believe in the vision, even when it's not profitable or popular. These individuals stick through the hard times, contribute ideas, and celebrate during the good times. Larry Page and Sergey Brin of Google or Steve Jobs and Steve Wozniak of Apple are examples of business partners who weathered storms together to build tech empires.

4. **True Friends During Financial Hardships:** On the path to financial freedom, there might be moments of doubt, or even financial setbacks. A true friend who offers encouragement during these times, or possibly even financial assistance without judgment, can be a crucial ally. Their faith in your abilities can help reignite your own.

5. **Networking Allies:** In any industry, there are those individuals who genuinely champion your cause. They might introduce you to the right people, speak highly of you in circles of influence, or offer guidance based on their experiences. These are not just casual networking contacts but true allies in your professional journey.

In summary, while individual effort and decision-making are vital, the journey towards wealth, financial freedom, and success is often influenced by the people around us. Recognizing and cherishing these 'keepers' is not just good for emotional well-being but can have tangible benefits in the quest for success.

Your financial triumphs will guide others through their challenges

One day you will tell your story of how you overcame what you went through and it will be someone else's survival guide.

This statement accentuates the transformative power of personal experiences, especially the struggles faced on the journey to success. By sharing these stories, individuals not only inspire but provide practical insights to others who might be walking a similar path.

ELABORATION:

Everyone faces challenges, whether in business, personal finance, or life in general. These challenges can often feel insurmountable. However, when one triumphs over these obstacles, their story becomes a testament to perseverance, adaptability, and resilience. Sharing such stories serves dual purposes: it's cathartic for the individual and educational (even life-changing) for the listener.

EXAMPLES:

1. **Business Failures Turned Successes:** Consider the story of Howard Schultz, the driving force behind Starbucks. Schultz's vision for Starbucks wasn't readily accepted. He faced rejections and had to buy Starbucks from its original owners. Now, his journey, filled with ups and downs, serves as an inspirational tale for many budding entrepreneurs, emphasizing the importance of belief in one's vision.

2. **Personal Financial Recovery:** There are countless stories of individuals who've faced bankruptcy or immense debt but managed to navigate their way out and achieve financial stability or even abundance. Their tales of budgeting, frugality, and financial planning can provide concrete steps for others facing similar financial woes.

3. **Investment Strategies:** Warren Buffett is known for his unique investment strategy, which contrasts with the high-paced trading many associate with the stock market. His emphasis on long-term, value-driven investment is now legendary. By sharing his principles and approach, many have found a more grounded way to approach stock investments.

4. **Overcoming Personal Barriers:** Oprah Winfrey faced poverty, abuse, and numerous personal and professional challenges. Today, her life story is not only inspirational but also provides tangible lessons on perseverance, seizing opportunities, and leveraging one's unique strengths.

5. **Learning from Mistakes:** Many financially successful individuals have, at some point, made significant financial blunders. By being open about these mistakes, they serve as cautionary tales, helping others avoid similar pitfalls.

In essence, the journey to wealth and financial freedom is seldom smooth. It's riddled with challenges, mistakes, and learning moments. However, these very experiences, when shared, become invaluable life lessons for others. They inspire, caution, guide, and, most importantly, offer hope – showcasing that with the right mindset and strategies, challenges can be overcome. It's in these shared stories that many find their roadmap to success.